Other books by Lois Lowry:

Switcharound

Your Move, J.P.!

Anastasia Krupnik

Anastasia Again!

Autumn Street

The Silent Boy

Just the Tates!

Book 1

The One Hundredth Thing About Caroline

by LOIS LOWRY

HOUGHTON MIFFLIN HARCOURT

BOSTON NEW YORK

For information about permission to reproduce selections from this book, write
to trade.permissions@hmhco.com or to Permissions, Houghton Mifflin Harcourt
Publishing Company, 3 Park Avenue, 19th Floor, New York, New York 10016.

hmhco.com
Book design by Rebecca Bond
The text of this book is set in Adobe Garamond.

The Library of Congress has cataloged the hardcover edition as follows:
Lowry, Lois.
The one hundredth thing about Caroline.
Summary: When their mother starts to date the mystery man on the fifth floor who
has been instructed by his agent to "eliminate the children" by the first of May,
eleven-year-old Caroline and her older brother figure they're targeted to be the
victims of a savage crime.
[1. Single-parent family — Fiction. 2. Brothers and sisters — Fiction.] I. Title.
PZ7.L9673On 1983 [Fic] 83–12629

ISBN: 978-0-395-34829-1 hardcover
ISBN: 978-1-328-75057-0 paperback

Manufactured in the United States of America
DOC 10 9 8 7 6 5 4 3 2 1
4500695177

For Michael Small
Good sport from People *magazine*

ONE

"CAN'T I EVEN HAVE DESSERT?" called Caroline Tate through her bedroom door.

"If you'd just try a *bite* of your dinner, Caroline. You wouldn't have to eat all of it," her mother called back.

"Just a bite," called her brother, "of this delicious, gray, cold squishy eggplant!"

"I wasn't talking to *you*, Beastly!"

Caroline's brother was named James Priestly Tate. Most people called him J.P. Caroline called him Beastly, and she really thought he was: beastly

beastly beastly. J.P. was thirteen, and even her mother admitted that thirteen was a beastly age.

Eleven felt pretty beastly too, Caroline decided, when you were sent to your room at half-past eight on a Friday night, just because you wouldn't taste your dinner.

Her mother opened her bedroom door and poked her head inside.

"Caroline, if you'd just try one *bite*. It's the principle of the thing."

"I *hate* it. I hate the way it looks, and I hate the way it smells. It's too horrible to talk about. Horrible horrible horrible. Anyway, Mom, psychologists all say that you should never force children to eat. Especially eggplant."

Her mother sighed. "Well, maybe psychologists can all afford steak every night. I, however, had to pay the dentist's bill out of this week's paycheck. And eggplant was on sale at the supermarket."

"What's dessert?"

"Jell-O."

"What color?"

"Red."

Caroline made a face. Red Jell-O wasn't worth eating eggplant for. Green Jell-O, maybe. But not red.

"Tell Beastly he can have mine. And I hope he chokes."

Her mother sighed again. "Well, good night then, Caroline. Be sure to brush your teeth."

The door closed. Caroline flopped on her bed and groaned. Eight-thirty on a Friday night, and she couldn't even watch television. Usually she was allowed to stay up until ten, if it wasn't a school night—sometimes even later, if there was an especially good movie on TV.

Well, at least tomorrow was Saturday, and Saturdays were always interesting. There was so much to do. Caroline reached for the calendar on her desk; she always listed her plans on the calendar.

At the top of the space under Saturday's date she had written: *HW.* She wrote that in every Saturday's space; it meant Housework. Her mother worked all week at the bank, so on Saturday mornings Caroline and J.P. helped her clean the apartment. It wasn't so bad. It was a small apartment. Beastly J.P. always ran the vacuum cleaner, because he liked machinery. And he was responsible for household repairs. Even Caroline had to admit that Beastly was something of a genius when it came to taking apart toasters and faucets and mixers.

Her mother cleaned the oven, which no one else wanted to do because the oven-cleaning stuff smelled terrible and stung your hands. Joanna Tate also did the marketing, which was why they sometimes had things like eggplant for dinner. Caroline and J.P. weren't allowed to do the marketing, because they would buy frozen pizza and chocolate eclairs, which cost too much and also, their mother said, weren't healthy.

Caroline always did the laundry. No one else *liked* doing the laundry, but Caroline loved it. Every Saturday morning she loaded all the dirty clothes into pillowcases, put them into the shopping cart, and went off to the laundromat on the corner with a pocketful of quarters.

The laundromat smelled of bleach, and a gray and white cat lived there. Interesting people came into the place. An old woman who had once been an opera singer came in sometimes on Saturday mornings, and sang arias while her wash was in the machine. Once a pair of grown-up identical twin men came in, wearing matching clothes; when they folded their clean laundry, Caroline could see that *all* of their clothes matched, even their pajamas and undershorts.

It took an hour and a half to get the laundry done, and you couldn't leave while it was in the machines, because someone might steal it. Laundry theft was one of the hazards of living in New York City. Caroline's father, who lived in Des Moines, said it would never happen there — but how the heck would he know, Caroline wondered, when he and his wife had a washer and dryer right in their dumb split-level house, and never set foot in a laundromat at all?

Next on her calendar, under *HW*, it said *MNH*. That stood for the Museum of Natural History. Caroline went there every Saturday, as regularly as she went to the laundromat; it was her favorite place in the whole city. Her mother had given her a membership in the Museum of Natural History for her birthday several years ago and had renewed it every year.

So Caroline had a special membership card, which she carried in her wallet, and when she showed it to the guard at the entrance, she didn't have to pay an admission fee. She got all of their special mailings for members, telling her of each new exhibit. And when she had enough money, which was not often, she could eat lunch in the special members' cafeteria. J.P. had thought it was a dumb birthday present. But it wasn't. It was the best birthday present Caroline had ever had. She had made friends with every single guard in the Museum of Natural History; they all knew her name and said, "Good morning, Caroline," when she came in. Mr. Erwitt, who had an office just inside the front door, called her "Unofficial Assistant Curator of Dinosaurs" and said she should apply for a job there when she got older. And upstairs, Gregor Keretsky, a world-renowned vertebrate paleontologist, was her very best adult friend.

Stacy Baurichter was her best eleven-year-old friend, and *Call Stacy* was written on her calendar as well. Stacy was in Caroline's class at the Burke-Thaxter School. Sometimes they saw each other on weekends, but not often, because Stacy lived on the other side of the city and you had to change buses twice.

Stacy Baurichter wanted to be an investigative reporter when she grew up. Caroline intended to be a vertebrate paleontologist, specializing in dinosaurs of the Mesozoic Era, but she was interested in investigative reporting, and sometimes she and Stacy worked on projects together.

Right now they were doing investigative studies of their apartment buildings. Caroline's investigation was easier than Stacy's for a couple of reasons. One, Caroline's building was smaller. It was a tall, thin house with five floors. Caroline's family lived on the third floor. So she was investigating the other four floors and making notes about the people who lived there. It was pretty easy, because she knew all of the other people quite well, except for the mystery man who had moved into the fifth floor in the fall.

Stacy lived in a very large building with twenty-six apartments, a doorman, and an electronic security system. So Stacy's job was much harder. But then Stacy was the one who had thought up the project to begin with.

The other reason that Caroline's investigation was easier was that Caroline's family was not rich. The other people in her building were not rich either. But Stacy's father was a senior partner in Bentley, Baurichter, and Bernstein, Attorneys-at-Law. Her family was quite rich, and all of the people in their apartment building were quite rich, and some of them were even famous, like Harrison Ledyard, the author who lived in 8-B and had won a Pulitzer Prize last year.

Rich people seemed to be a little suspicious of Stacy's investigative questions. So she was having a bit of trouble compiling information and was starting to use stealthier methods than simple conversations. But she said that was a challenge, and investigative reporters welcomed challenges.

Caroline understood that, because there would be a lot of challenges in dinosaur work as well.

On Caroline's calendar, she had written, finally, *IMM*. Investigate Mystery Man. She wasn't at all sure how she would go about that; sometimes she passed him on the stairs, hurrying up to his fifth-floor apartment, and sometimes he would nod at her, bobbing his head up and down in an awkward way. But he never spoke to her. Maybe tomorrow she could start a conversation about whether the hall light bulbs needed changing, and then she could casually ask him about his past, his future, his hopes, his dreams, his fears.

Caroline set her calendar on the table beside her bed. She stood by the window and looked down into the back yard behind their building. It wasn't much of a back yard, really; it was simply a small fenced area surrounded by other buildings, and now, at night, lights from the downstairs apartments cast illuminated rectangles across the bare earth and the straggly bushes that were trying hard to acknowledge April by growing a green leaf here and there.

Someone once, long ago, had tried to create a real yard, and had planted the few bushes and set out some wrought-iron chairs. But now most of the bushes had died and the others had grown out of control; the chairs had been tipped over and never righted again. A workman had once left behind a paper bag filled with lunch; cats had come in over the fence and eaten the sandwich, but the remains of the forgotten lunch were still there: the faded bag, torn waxed paper, and a rusty thermos on its side.

Caroline sighed. It wasn't a yard that would ever be photographed for *Apartment Life* magazine. But there were hints there of other people's lives, lives that had moved on someplace else. She wondered if deep down, under the scruffy yard, under the tunnels of the New York subway system, which rumbled beneath the streets and buildings and yards, under the sewers and the buried electrical lines, there might be bones and fossils, hints of the life that had existed long ago in time.

She took off her clothes, dropped them on the floor—tomorrow was laundry day, after all—and put on her pajamas. She thought about brushing her teeth, but going to the bathroom meant walking through the living room of the apartment, and that meant walking past Beastly, who had eaten the eggplant without complaint and was now watching TV. She decided to brush her teeth twice in the morning to make up for skipping tonight.

Caroline got her stuffed Stegosaurus down from her closet shelf. She was careful never to let anyone

—particularly her brother—know that she still slept with a stuffed animal. Not even Stacy Baurichter, Investigative Reporter, knew that.

Not that it was just *any* stuffed animal. Stegosaurus was Caroline's favorite of all the dinosaurs. She felt sorry for him, because he was ugly and dumb. Scientists like Caroline knew that although the Stegosaurus had weighed two tons, his teeny brain was no bigger than a golf ball. And even though he had had a hundred teeth, they weren't very sharp ones, so he hadn't been able to eat other animals. He was just a clumsy and gentle plant-eater.

But, thought Caroline as she curled up with her arms around her Stegosaurus to go to sleep, even though he was a plant-eater with a two-ounce brain, he was probably smart enough to hate eggplant.

Two

"Don't put this blue blouse in with the white things, Caroline."

"*Mother,* for heaven's sake. I'm the laundry expert, remember? Of *course* I won't put the blue blouse in with the white things. Here, give it to me. It goes in this pile, with the jeans."

Joanna Tate chuckled. "That's the thirty-eighth thing I love about you, Caroline," she said. "Your laundry expertise."

"You're positive it isn't the thirty-seventh?"

"Nope. Thirty-seventh is your perpetual ability

to wake up cheerful on Saturday mornings. Very few people have that ability."

"I love Saturdays," said Caroline. "There's so much stuff to do."

Together they sorted the dirty clothes, put them into pillowcases, and loaded them into the wheeled shopping cart. Caroline thumped it down the stairs of their building—sometimes she wished they had an elevator, the way Stacy's building did—and stopped on the first floor to check the mail.

Most eleven-year-old people didn't get mail very often. But Caroline did, because she always sent away for free catalogues. Then her name was on mailing lists: Ms. C. Tate. There was always mail for Ms. C. Tate.

In addition, of course, her membership in the Museum of Natural History brought mail. Today there was a notice about a lecture on spiders; she saved that, even though she wouldn't be able to go because it was a school night. But she would write a note to the lecturer, Dr. Morton Schultz from the University of New Mexico, telling him that she was sorry she couldn't make it. She was moderately interested in spiders. Caroline had a subscription to *National Geographic,* which her father renewed every year as a Christmas gift, and she always read the articles about spiders, bees, and ants. Mountain-climbing expeditions didn't interest her much, because she didn't like being cold; and sailboat trips around the world didn't interest her much, because she didn't like being wet. But there was almost always an article about insects or archaeological projects. So she was able every year to write an honest and enthusiastic thank-you note to her father, in Des Moines, for *National Geographic.*

Her father didn't interest Caroline much, because he had moved to Des Moines when she was two years old and never wrote her any letters. She went to visit him now and then, and she liked his wife okay, but they made her babysit their little boy. If Caroline wanted to babysit, she didn't need to go all the way to Des Moines.

Also in the mail for Ms. C. Tate was a catalogue from Publishers Central Bureau, which she would read later. Reading the descriptions of books was always interesting, even though she never had the money to buy any.

And there was something telling her "Congratulations C. Tate you may have won the *Reader's Digest* Sweepstakes." When she was younger, she used to believe that. Now she just tossed it into the wastebasket by the mail slot. Some of the other people in the building had already picked up their mail, apparently, because there were two other *Reader's Digest* letters in the wastebasket.

Caroline leaned over and looked at the wastebasket more closely. It could be a good source for investigative reporting. Stacy spent a lot of time in the basement of her building, wearing rubber gloves so that she wouldn't leave fingerprints, going through the trash.

Sure enough, there were two crumpled pieces of mail addressed to Frederick Fiske.

She left her mother's mail—all bills, addressed to Ms. J. Tate—on the hall table. But she stuffed Frederick Fiske's two letters into a pocket of her jeans. Frederick Fiske was the Mystery Man who lived on the fifth floor.

Caroline thumped the laundry down the front steps and out to the sidewalk. Billy DeVito was playing on the sidewalk with two stones and a piece of string. Billy DeVito was five and lived on the first floor.

"Hi, Billy. How's it going?"

Billy wrinkled his nose and thought for a minute. Caroline liked Billy because he always took things very seriously, even things like "How's it going?"

"Good," he said, finally. "I got me this string. It busted last night when it was playing 'Lady of Spain.'"

Most people wouldn't have understood what Billy DeVito was talking about. But Caroline did, because she knew a lot about the DeVito family. Investigating them had been easy; Mrs. DeVito liked to talk. Her husband played the violin in a Hungarian restaurant. He gave his broken violin strings to Billy.

Mr. DeVito's violin had cost four thousand

dollars, and they had insurance on it. Mrs. DeVito had told Caroline once that she wished her husband's violin would be stolen; then the insurance company would pay them four thousand dollars and they could buy a new living room set, and Mr. DeVito could get a job in the post office or something, like a normal person.

She didn't really mean that, though. She liked it that Billy's father played the violin in the Little Hungary Café. Some nights he brought home left-over food and they would light candles and pretend they were eating in a restaurant themselves, and he would play "Night and Day" on his violin, just for her. Someone who worked in the post office could never do that for his wife.

Caroline walked on down to the laundromat on the corner. She loaded three machines, added detergent, put three quarters into each machine, and turned them on. The gray and white cat jumped down from the top of the dryer where he'd been sleeping, and rubbed against her leg, purring.

"Hi, Cheery," Caroline said, and scratched behind his ears.

No one knew whom the cat belonged to, or who fed him, or what his name really was. But the people who did their laundry at the laundromat all called him Cheery, because he liked to roll in the little piles of spilled detergent on the floor; then he would jump on top of the dryer and clean the detergent out of his whiskers and sneeze.

He didn't care what kind of detergent he rolled in. But it would have sounded stupid to call him All or Tide. So everybody called him New Blue Cheer. Cheery, for short.

Caroline glanced around to see who else was in the place this morning.

"Hello, Mrs. Kokolis," she called. "Are you starting to pack yet?"

Mrs. Kokolis smiled and kept on knitting. She was such a good knitter that she could talk and make complicated sweaters at the same time.

"Not yet," she said. "Soon, though."

Mr. and Mrs. Kokolis used to own the Greek restaurant across the street. They had come to the United States from Greece thirty years ago and had been saving, ever since their children grew up, to go back to Greece for a visit. Then Mr. Kokolis had died one day, very suddenly. He had been making stuffed grape leaves — his specialty — when he looked up, Mrs. Kokolis had told Caroline, and said, "Well. My goodness." Then he fell over and was dead, of a heart attack.

So Mrs. Kokolis was going to go back to Greece all alone. At least, she said she was. But she never quite got around to doing it. She kept canceling her airline reservations.

"Soon, though," she kept saying.

"In June," she said, today. "June for certain."

Caroline smiled at Mrs. Kokolis. She watched a man putting his clothes into a dryer. She giggled to herself. An Apatosaurus, she thought. He looks like an Apatosaurus.

It was true. He wasn't as *large* as an Apatosaurus, of course, because a real Apatosaurus would have filled *two* laundromats and still had to stick its head out through a window.

But he was very tall, with a long neck and a nose that looked too high on his face. He had buck teeth and a stupid look.

Caroline giggled again, remembering something. The Apatosaurus had two brains, both very small; so he wasn't at all smart. But his second brain was located in his bottom, right where his tail began.

The man putting his clothes into the dryer didn't have a tail, of course. And Caroline was fairly certain that he didn't have a second brain in his behind. But he sure looked like an Apatosaurus.

It was surprising, the number of people who resembled dinosaurs.

No one else was in the laundry this morning except for a couple of teenage girls reading magazines. Caroline checked to make sure that her laundry was going around in the washers. Then she sat down and took Frederick Fiske's mail out of her pocket.

She felt a little guilty, beginning to read it. But it was open, after all, and it had been in the wastebasket.

Anyway, investigators had to use any method possible to find out stuff. Stacy had reminded her of that often.

The first letter was simply boring. It was a note

from the public library, reminding him politely that a book he'd checked out, *Forensic Toxicology,* was a month overdue. Caroline didn't know what "forensic toxicology" meant; it didn't sound very interesting. She stuffed that letter back into her pocket.

Then she read the second letter, and her head began to whirl, the way her laundry was whirling now in the washing machine.

> *Fred,* [the letter began]:
> *The woman's terrific. But the kids, frankly, seem more and more of a problem.* Eliminate *the kids. You can figure out a way.*
> *Call me, and we'll have lunch and talk it over.*
> *Carl*

That was all. Caroline turned the envelope over and looked at the return address. Carl Broderick was the man's name, and he lived on East Fifty-Second Street.

Why would a man on East Fifty-Second Street be telling Frederick Fiske to murder some children?

Three

CAROLINE DIALED STACY'S NUMBER as soon as the laundry was folded and put away.

"Guess what, Stace?" she said.

"*You* guess what," said Stacy Baurichter. "Harrison Ledyard is having an affair."

"How do you know?"

"I looked through his trash. It was down in the basement of our building, because the superintendent hadn't put it outside yet. And there were cigarette butts with lipstick on them, and—"

"Stacy. Maybe his mother came to visit. Maybe

his mother smokes. Or his sister. Or his cleaning lady. You have to verify your evidence, Stacy."

"That's not all. Wait'll you hear." Stacy paused ominously. "There was something else. A bra."

"In his *trash?*"

"Ripped."

"A ripped bra?"

"Torn in a passionate frenzy. Honest. Now, don't try to make me believe *that* was his mother!"

"No," said Caroline, "I guess not. Was it black lace?"

"Pink. No lace, but some embroidery. Thirty-four B."

"That's not very big," said Caroline. "I think for a passionate frenzy you really need a thirty-eight D at least."

But Stacy assumed her investigative reporter's voice. "Research indicates that ever since Brooke Shields became so popular, small boobs are in."

"Stacy, *in* is one thing. Passionate frenzy is something else."

"Well. Anyway. It's the first interesting thing I've found out about Harrison Ledyard in all these months. Can you imagine? He looks so quiet and intellectual and Pulitzer Prize–winning. And now it turns out that in his spare time he's grabbing and ripping and tearing the clothes off innocent women. I made a lot of notes. The bra's a Maidenform. And the lipstick is Misty Coral, I think. The cigarettes are Benson and Hedges menthol."

"Stacy, for a minute I almost forgot what I wanted to tell you. It's even better than Harrison Ledyard's sex life."

"What could be better than *that?*"

Caroline looked around to be certain no one could overhear her. She had taken the telephone into the bathroom, but the door wouldn't close tight over the cord. J.P. was in his bedroom, probably working on an electrical project. Her mother was washing the kitchen floor, and the radio was on in the kitchen. She eased the door closed again as far as it would go and spoke in a low voice.

"Frederick Fiske," she whispered into the telephone.

"The guy upstairs? He's having an affair, too?"

"Yes. But worse than that."

"Baurichter Demands Details," said Stacy. When she was excited about something, she often spoke in headlines. It was part of her journalistic training.

"He's a murderer," announced Caroline.

"A *what?* How do you know? Did you find body parts in his trash?"

"The murder hasn't taken place yet," Caroline explained. "But I found a letter. He's *going* to commit a murder. And guess what kind?"

"Ax?"

"No, it doesn't say the method. But it's going to be a *child* murder. A *children* murder, actually. The letter said, 'Eliminate the kids.'"

"Save it for fingerprints," ordered Stacy, "Prints Often Prove Case," she added, in a headline.

"Too late," said Caroline. "I picked it up in my bare hands already. Anyway, it doesn't matter. I know who wrote it, and I know who it was to."

"Well, save it for evidence. And take notes. Listen: this is important, Caroline. Do friends describe him as a loner?"

"What?"

"In the newspapers," Stacy explained, "after they catch a psychopathic killer, it always says, 'Friends described him as a loner.' Do Frederick Fiske's friends describe him as a loner?"

"*Stacy*," Caroline pointed out impatiently, "I don't even know if he *has* any friends. He's always by himself."

"That proves it, then."

"Proves what?"

"He's a loner," said Stacy.

"Stace," Caroline whispered suddenly, "I have to go. My mother's coming.

"See you at school Monday," she said cheerfully, and loudly, into the phone as her mother passed in the hallway. "Bye, Stacy."

J.P. came out of his bedroom. "Bye, Stacy," he imitated, in a high, girlish voice. His own voice was beginning to deepen.

"Creep," said Caroline to her brother.

"Guess what I'm building in my room," said J.P.

"Couldn't care less."

"An electrifier," he announced happily. "Some-time, when you least expect it, when you're sound asleep, I'm going to sneak into your bedroom and —"

"MOM!" yelled Caroline.

Her mother sighed. She had curled up on the living room couch with a magazine. "He's only kidding, Caroline," she said. "James, stop teasing your sister."

"Zap," said J.P. meaningfully, looking sinister.

"Go zap yourself, Beastly," said Caroline with disdain. She went into her room and closed the door.

In her bedroom, Caroline knelt on her freshly made bed (Saturday was the only day that she didn't have to make her own bed; her mother changed the sheets on Saturday), reached up to the bookcase attached to the wall, and took down a dictionary. She rarely used her dictionary. It was wedged in so tightly that when she removed it, three mystery books and a fat volume about the Paleolithic Age came crashing down, bounced on her blue bedspread, and fell to the floor. Caroline glanced at them, shrugged, and left them there. Sometimes, in the house-decorating magazines that her mother liked to read, there were books scattered on the floor of a room. It gave a room a casual, intellectual look. Caroline decided that her room could have a casual, intellectual look until next Saturday, when it was cleaning day again.

She took Frederick Fiske's mail out of her pocket. The letter from Carl Broderick didn't require a dictionary. It was quite clear: a clear command to "eliminate the kids." No words to look up there. "Eliminate the kids" meant murder them, and you didn't need a dictionary to figure *that* out.

It was the other letter that was more puzzling. She had simply brushed it aside when she'd read it the first time. A notice from the library about an overdue book. Caroline got notices like that all the time. Once she had kept a book on vertebrate paleontology so long that the fine was $2.50; she had had to use some of her grandmother's birthday check to pay off that fine. She could almost have *bought* a book about vertebrate paleontology for that amount.

But now she looked carefully at Frederick Fiske's notice from the library. She realized that if the police ever examined the library records for Caroline

MacKenzie Tate, they would be able to figure out quite a bit about her. They would find a few teen-age romances and one or two books about good grooming that she had checked out last year, when she had begun to be interested in a boy at school and thought that maybe if she changed her hairstyle and maybe used eye makeup he would notice her. He hadn't. She had tried three different hairstyles with no effect at all on the boy. And her mother had said no, absolutely not, not until you are *much* older, to the eye makeup.

The police might also think that she was briefly interested in breeding cocker spaniels or something, but that would be a mistake. It had to do with the eye makeup and hairstyles. She had taken out a book called *Grooming a Dog* by mistake.

But mostly they would find that she had checked out books about prehistoric eras, extinct mammals, fossils, reptiles, and paleontology. They would be able to figure out from them that Caroline was more interested in being a paleontologist than she was in eye makeup or in raising champion dogs.

So it was definitely one way to figure out what

Frederick Fiske was interested in. She looked at the letter from the library again. The overdue book was called *Forensic Toxicology*. She didn't know what either word meant.

Forensic meant, she found from the dictionary, "pertaining to legal proceedings."

Well. *That* was interesting. If Frederick Fiske intended to start murdering children, there were certainly going to be legal proceedings.

Actually, Caroline thought, she really had to give him credit. It was pretty clever to read a book about legal proceedings *before* he murdered anyone.

She checked the library letter again and searched through the dictionary for the second word, *Toxicology*. When she found it, her eyes widened. She read the definition twice to be sure it said what she thought it said.

"Toxicology (tok'si-kol'o-ji) *n.* (toxic + logy). (See TOXIC.) The science of poisons."

It was horrible. Horrible horrible horrible. It made Caroline think vaguely of eggplant. She shuddered, and put the dictionary away.

It confirmed what she had already known, down

deep. "Eliminate the kids" could, conceivably, have meant send them off to live with their father in Des Moines. Every now and then, Caroline's mother threatened to do just that, usually when Caroline and J.P. had been fighting a lot. Once, at the end of a long rainy Sunday, when Caroline and J.P. had been at war all day, they ran through the apartment throwing ice cubes at each other. The whole fight had started over ice cubes. Caroline had poured herself a ginger ale that morning, and she had said to her brother sarcastically, "It sure is nice to find ice cubes in the refrigerator occasionally," because usually he never refilled the ice trays.

J.P. had just looked at her in a fake friendly sort of way while she drank half the glass of ginger ale. Then he had said, casually, "I spit in the trays before I put them in the freezer."

By the end of the day, their fight had escalated into major warfare, with ice cubes as weapons. Finally their mother had thrown down the book she was reading and shouted, "That's *it!* If you two don't stop it this *instant,* I am sending you both to Des Moines to live with your father!"

It was the sort of thing parents said once in a while. But Frederick Fiske wasn't a parent. He lived alone on the fifth floor. No children ever came to visit, Caroline was quite sure.

And the library book cinched it. An angry parent might be tempted to send a bratty child to Des Moines, but an angry parent would never start studying up on the science of poisons. Eggplant, maybe. Not poisons.

Only a murderer would do that.

Four

"WHAT IS ALL THIS secret telephoning?" asked Mrs. Tate. "You're not in any kind of trouble, are you, Caroline?"

"No," said Caroline casually. "I'm just calling Stacy about an assignment."

That wasn't a lie. She took the telephone into the bathroom, closed the door as far as she could over the cord, and said loudly, when Stacy answered, "Hi, Stacc. I'm calling you about an assignment."

Then she lowered her voice. "Listen, Stace, it's

not a school assignment. I just wanted my mother to think that it was. It's a detective assignment."

"About the murderer?" Stacy was whispering, too, although she didn't need to. Stacy had her very own private telephone, in her bedroom. It was yellow, to match the decorator bedspreads and curtains. There were some really good things about being rich.

"Yeah. Can you go out this afternoon? It's not very far."

"Sure. I'll just tell my mother I'm going to the art museum. She always thinks it's terrific that I go to the art museum all the time."

"I didn't know you did."

"I don't. Half the time I'm down in the basement going through the trash. But I can't tell my mother *that*."

"Well, listen. I want you to go to East Fifty-Second Street. That's not far, is it?"

"Nope. I can get the bus at the corner and be there in twenty minutes. Or I can jog and be there in ten."

"Whichever. Anyway, it's important." Caroline

took Carl Broderick's letter out of her pocket and read the name and address to Stacy. "Just check it out, would you? He's an accomplice. He may be the mastermind, in fact."

"What should I look for?"

"I don't know," Caroline whispered. "Just see what's at that address. Probably it won't be a Poisoning Center, or anything. But there might be clues. Look for clues."

"Gotcha. I'll call you back in, say, an hour or so."

"Right."

"Caroline," Stacy said ominously before she hung up, "if no one ever hears from me again, give that address to the police, would you? They'll find my body there."

"Right. But don't take any dangerous chances, Stacy."

"I won't. But if after, oh, three days, say, I don't return—"

"I will, Stacy. I promise. But be careful. Remember, it's *children* they're after."

"I'll wear lipstick," said Stacy. "I got some

Crimson Shadows lipstick at the drugstore, just for assignments like this."

"Stacy's calling back in about an hour," said Caroline when she went to the kitchen for lunch. "She's doing some research for an assignment we have together."

"Fine," said her mother cheerfully. "Want a pickle with your sandwich?"

Caroline and J.P. each took a dill pickle.

"The phone may not be working in an hour," announced Caroline's brother. "I'm going to do some experiments on it after lunch."

"Don't. Touch. That. Phone," said Caroline angrily, with a mouth full of bologna sandwich.

"She's absolutely right, James," said Mrs. Tate. "The phone company said they were going to charge for the repairs next time you experimented with the telephone."

"Well," said J.P., chewing, "can I borrow your radio, then? I need to experiment with *something*."

His mother sighed. "All right. You can use my radio. But don't wreck the alarm, okay? I can't be late to work Monday. I was late twice last week, once because you ruined my toothbrush, James—"

"I had to clean the gunk out of my motor with *something*," J.P. explained.

"—and once because I couldn't find my pocketbook."

Caroline sighed. "I already said I was sorry, Mom. I was examining the alligator skin under a magnifying glass, and somehow it ended up under a whole pile of stuff on my desk."

"It isn't alligator, anyway. It's plastic. That pocketbook only cost fourteen dollars. If I lose my job because I'm late one more time, I won't even be able to afford a *plastic* pocketbook. I'll have to become a bag lady."

"I'll support you in your old age, Mom," said Caroline. "After I'm a paleontologist, I'll send you a check every month, from Asia Minor or wherever I am."

"Me too," said J.P. "When I'm an electrical engineer, I'll be really rich."

"Maybe by then I will have married a millionaire," said their mother. "In the meantime, do either of you want another sandwich, bearing in mind that this bologna cost one eighty-nine a pound?"

"Me," said J.P.

"Pig," said Caroline sweetly, and ducked just in time to evade the dill pickle that her brother threw at her.

"Sometimes," sighed their mother, "I wish that I had remained childless."

Back in her room, waiting for Stacy to call, Caroline curled up on her bed with her stuffed Stegosaurus. She began to think about dinosaurs in general, and about the particular contribution that she would make to science after she was a qualified paleontologist.

Caroline had begun to develop the Tate Theory of Evolution. According to her theory, certain people alive in the twentieth century had not actually evolved very much from prehistoric times. Of course, they were disguised as civilized people, because they wore clothes and held jobs and went to school and did all the things that civilized people are supposed to do.

But the man at the laundromat was a good example. He really had been very much like the buck-toothed Apatosaurus, with his nose too high on his face. Fortunately, old Apatosaurus was weak and dumb and harmless; probably that man would go home from the laundry and eat some lettuce and cucumbers for lunch, since Apatosaurus was a plant-eater. He wasn't a danger to society, but he was a good example of Caroline's theory that some people arc little more than barely evolved dinosaurs. She was surprised that no scientists had noticed it yet.

James Priestly Tate, for example. Talk about a creepy-crawler. Her brother was a perfect example of a practically unchanged Coelophysis. Small, skinny, with a rat face and lousy posture. Little clawlike hands and a terrible disposition. And a carnivore, to boot. J.P. had gnawed into that second bologna sandwich as if there was no tomorrow, just the way a Coelophysis would. J.P. even ate eggplant.

And now—Caroline thought about her Tate

Theory again — there was Frederick Fiske. Extremely tall. Big head, with a grin all the time. When she had first begun to notice Frederick Fiske, after he moved in upstairs, she had thought his grin was just the kind of indiscriminate friendliness that some adults display. Now she knew differently. Now she knew why that grin was familiar. It went with his tall body and his long strides. Probably concealed behind that grin was a whole mouthful of steak-knife teeth.

She recognized all of the symptoms. They belonged to the most terrible dinosaur of all, the one that a book she had read described as having a completely sinister pattern of life. It was the kind of life that she now knew Frederick Fiske was leading. The author had described it as: Hunt. Kill. Eat. Sleep. Hunt. Kill. Etc.

She was quite, quite sure now that her theory was correct, and that Frederick Fiske was, in truth, little more than an unevolved *Tyrannosaurus rex*.

The Great Killer.

When the telephone rang half an hour later, Caroline jumped up to answer it. Her mother had gone out to the grocery store, and J.P. was in his room, busily removing all the inside parts of Joanna Tate's clock radio.

Stacy was breathless. "I jogged," she said, panting. "All the way there and all the way back. I stepped in one dog mess and almost got hit by a taxi. But I'm safe, except my left shoe stinks."

"What did you find out?"

"Let me get my breath." Stacy panted for a minute. "Yuck," she said, finally. "Now that I can breathe normally, I can really smell my shoe."

"Take it off."

"Hold on a minute." There was a very long silence while Caroline held the phone and waited. Finally Stacy came back.

"Okay," she said. "I scraped it off into the trashmasher. Now, Caroline, listen. This is really bigger than both of us."

"What do you mean? Come on, Stacy, tell me what you found out!"

"Your guy Frederick Fiske? He's not just your ordinary murderer. He's part of a *ring*. Probably international."

"Stacy. How do you know? What did you *find?*"

"Well, like you said, it wasn't an office called Poison, Limited, or anything. It was just an apartment house, with a doorman."

"Oh, rats. So you couldn't get in. Doormen are such snots."

"That's not true, Caroline. You just think that because you've never had one. *We* have a doorman, so I know how to deal with them."

"What did you do?" asked Caroline.

"First, after I saw that it was an apartment building with a doorman, I went back around the corner and wiped off all the Crimson Shadows lipstick. I didn't want him to think I was a hooker or anything."

"Then what?"

"Then I put on my most innocent face. You know that face I can do, with my eyes all wide and everything?"

"Yeah."

"I did that face. And I went right up to the doorman and in my innocent voice—you know the one?"

"Yeah. High and babyish."

"Right. And in that voice, I said, 'Please, could I have the correct spelling of Mr. Broderick's name? I have to write him a letter for a school project, and if I don't spell it correctly I won't get a good grade.'"

"Big deal, so he spelled it for you."

"Caroline," said Stacy patiently, "doormen don't spell. He opened the door and he watched me while I went over to the mailboxes and copied it. I had my investigative notebook with me, of course."

"Stacy, I could have spelled it for you. I have it right here on the letter."

Stacy sighed an exasperated sigh. "Caroline, you'll never be a great investigator. I didn't care about the spelling. I was looking for *clues*."

"How on earth can you find clues on a mailbox?"

There was a dramatic pause. Then Stacy said, "Right there on the mailbox, it said 'CARL BRODERICK, AGENT.'"

"*Agent?*"

"So you see."

"See what? He could be a *real estate* agent!"

"Does a real estate agent tell his clients to kill children?"

Caroline thought. "Maybe if an apartment listing says 'No pets or children.'"

"Come on. Face the facts."

"You're right," said Caroline. "You're absolutely right. It's a murder ring of some sort."

"Is there anything else you want me to do?"

"No," said Caroline thoughtfully. "I really have to sort things out. I'll call you."

"Okay," said Stacy. "I'll be here. I'm going to type up these notes."

"Stacy, don't leave your notes lying around where anyone can find them."

"Are you kidding?" asked Stacy. "Caroline, I'm not a newcomer to this field. I type in code."

FIVE

"I'M GOING TO THE Museum of Natural History, Mom," said Caroline after she had talked to Stacy.

Her mother was putting groceries away in the refrigerator. She looked startled when Caroline came into the kitchen, and then guilty. She stood awkwardly in front of the table, as if she were trying to hide something. Caroline looked at her suspiciously for a moment.

"Did you buy another eggplant?" she asked.

"No, of course not," said her mother. She began to hum a little tune. A sure sign of some sort of guilt.

"What is it, then?" Caroline lunged forward suddenly and got past her mother, who tried a football blocking maneuver. But she moved to the right; Caroline moved to the left, past her, and took a good look at the kitchen table.

Eggs. It wasn't eggs. Caroline liked eggs. Bread. That was okay. Hamburger. Nothing wrong with hamburger.

Then she saw it. Them. Two lumpy, repulsive, no-color things lying on the table side by side. Like something you would look away from if you saw it lying in a gutter.

"All right, Mom," said Caroline. "What *are* they?"

"They're good," said her mother. "I have this recipe—"

"What *are* they?"

"Parsnips," said her mother.

"*Parsnips! Mom!* Nobody makes their kids eat parsnips! Listen, before you do another thing, Mom, call the Hotline for Child Abuse. Confess to them that you were planning to feed parsnips to your children. They're there to *help* you, Mom."

"Look," said her mother hastily, picking up a

cookbook. "This recipe says you cook them with orange juice and brown sugar. It's called Candied Parsnips."

"*Mom,*" wailed Caroline.

"I know," her mother said dejectedly, sitting down in a kitchen chair. "But J.P. will like them. He eats anything."

"So does any Coelophysis," Caroline pointed out.

But her mother didn't pay any attention to that. "Caroline," she said, "they only cost forty-nine cents."

Caroline groaned. "Mom, you have to find a millionaire to marry very soon. Otherwise we're all going to die of starvation or malnutrition or dysentery or something."

"Hey—" Her mother brightened. "You said Stacy wanted you to eat at her house sometime this week."

"Right. What night are you planning Candied You-Know?"

"Monday?"

"Okay. Monday night I'll eat at the Baurichters'. You and J.P. can have a parsnip orgy without me."

"Agreed. They may not taste too bad, actually."

Caroline made a face. "You know, Mom, if you'd just go to some of the lectures at the Museum of Natural History, I *know* you'd meet a terrific man. Probably one who can afford pork chops and steak—"

But her mother sighed. "Caroline, I can't bear to hear about spiders and things. I get queasy."

It was true. Caroline's mother couldn't even look at a *National Geographic,* for fear there might be snakes or lizards or insects inside.

She *had* tried some other methods for meeting Mr. Right, even though she absolutely refused to go to singles bars. She said she was too old for that; she was already thirty-four. Also, she was afraid she might meet stranglers at singles bars, and Caroline thought she might be right about that.

First, she had joined the Gourmet Eating Club. But after six weeks it was a disaster. She had gained fifteen pounds, none of her clothes fit, and all of the men she had met at the Gourmet Eating Club had ended up dating each other.

Then—after a diet to lose the fifteen pounds

—she had joined the New York Scrabble Players Society. Actually, Joanna Tate was pretty good at Scrabble. She *always* beat Caroline. And she had enjoyed the weekly Scrabble tournaments. More important, she had met a man. He seemed to have an okay job—he was a stockbroker or something—and he wasn't bad-looking, although he wore glasses so thick that his eyes always looked huge, as if you were seeing them through a magnifying glass.

He knew eighty-two two-letter words. That was the problem. He took Scrabble very seriously. He took Caroline's mother out for dinner one night, after taking her for coffee several evenings after Scrabble tournaments. Caroline waited up until her mother got home at eleven-thirty, just to find out how the evening had gone.

"Boorring," said Caroline's mother.

"Why? What did you talk about?"

"Ut," said her mother, kicking off her shoes. "Ai. Jo. Re. Ti. Li."

"Mom, why are you talking so weird?" Caroline had asked.

"I'm not. That's what we talked about. Two-letter

Scrabble words. He wants me to memorize this list. He wrote it up especially for me." She groaned and handed Caroline a neatly typed list on a piece of yellow paper.

"And that's all?"

"Of course not. There are seventy-six others. Xi. Pi. Eh. Ah. Fa . . ."

And she groaned again, picked up her shoes, and went off to her bedroom, muttering two-letter words. Caroline didn't blame her for never going out with him again.

Her mother put the parsnips into the refrigerator, sighed, and poured herself a cup of coffee.

"Better wear your raincoat if you're going to the museum," she said. "It looks like rain. Your brother said his barometer is falling or rising or something."

Caroline made a face and got her raincoat out of the hall closet. She loaded her bookbag with paper and pencils for her museum research and left the apartment. Much as she hated to admit it, J.P. was right: the sky was dark with storm clouds, and a wind had come up, scattering litter across the streets and sidewalks in puffy gusts.

The museum wasn't a long walk. Caroline headed east to Central Park, and then south to Seventy-Ninth Street, where the enormous building covered the entire block.

In front of the museum, next to the huge statue of Theodore Roosevelt, a boy was unwrapping a candy bar. He dropped the wrapper on the museum steps.

"Excuse me," Caroline said to him politely, and pointed to the nearby sign: LITTERING IS FILTHY AND SELFISH. SO DON'T DO IT.

The boy looked at her for a moment. Then very carefully he reached into his pocket, removed a wadded-up tissue, and dropped it ostentatiously next to his candy wrapper. He grinned nastily and sauntered off.

Caroline looked around for a policeman. But there were only two nuns, a taxidriver leaning against his parked cab, and a couple of mothers with a troop of Brownies.

She thought about making a citizen's arrest. But the boy was bigger than she — he looked at least fifteen — and besides, he was already down at the corner of Seventy-Eighth Street.

She sighed and picked up his trash with two fingers. It was almost as bad as touching parsnips. She dropped it into a trash can angrily and headed up the steps into the museum.

"Hello, Mr. Erwitt," she called into the office inside the front door. Mr. Erwitt looked up from his desk and waved.

"Hello there, Caroline," he called back. "Great exhibit in Meteorites, Minerals, and Gems this afternoon!"

"Thanks anyway, Mr. Erwitt," she said. "I have work to do on the fourth floor."

She showed her membership card to the woman at the admissions booth, took the little blue button that indicated she hadn't sneaked in, and attached it to her raincoat. Then she walked past the postcard counter and the gift shop, down the hall to the elevator.

The fourth floor was absolutely her favorite

place in the entire museum. No question. Biology of Invertebrates, on the first floor, was okay; and so was Small Mammals. On the second floor, African Mammals was kind of interesting because of the stuffed elephants and the gorilla who looked like King Kong and had a leaf sticking out of his mouth to indicate that he was a harmless plant-eater. Primates, on the third floor, wasn't too bad.

But the fourth floor was heaven. The Hall of Early Dinosaurs even had blue walls, which was what Caroline had always supposed heaven had.

She went into the blue-walled Early Dinosaur room and stood there, awed, as she always was. There, in the center, were the Stegosaurus, the Allosaurus, and the gigantic Brontosaurus—only their bones, of course—standing in their huge, awkward poses.

"Hi, you guys," said Caroline. She thought of them as old buddies. She always came in to say hi, even when she was going to the Late Dinosaur exhibit, as she was today.

They all smiled their toothy smiles at her. Even Allosaurus, a fierce flesh-eater, looked sweet and happy and a little embarrassed, standing there without his skin, quite helpless.

Then she went over to say hi to the mummified Anatosaurus in his glass case. They had found him in Wyoming, of all places, with his skin still on. Sometimes Caroline wished her father had moved to Wyoming instead of Des Moines; she would be tempted to visit him more often if he had. There might be a mummified Anatosaurus buried in his back yard.

Finally, she walked to the end of the huge room and said, "Greetings, Jaws," to the jaws of the giant extinct shark that hung at the entrance to the room of Fossil Fishes.

The jaws just hung there, wide open, as if they were waiting for a dentist to say "Spit."

Caroline wasn't all that crazy about the shark jaws. They gave her the creeps. But she always said "Greetings" to them, politely, before she left the Hall of Early Dinosaurs. She did it for the same reason that she was always very nice to Marcia-Anne Hennessy, the worst bully in her class at school.

She didn't want the giant shark jaws, or Marcia-Anne Hennessy, ever to take a dislike to her.

Then Caroline took out her notebook and headed to her destination: Late Dinosaurs. That room was just as big, though the walls were green. And in the center, dominating the Triceratops and the two Trach-odonts next to him, stood the hideous, monstrous *Tyrannosaurus rex*. Even without his skin, quite naked and with all his bones exposed, he was horrifying. It made Caroline shiver just to look at him. It also gave her a stiff neck, because he was so tall that she almost had to do a backbend to see his face towering above her, looking down, with his sharp teeth exposed. If ever, by magic, he should come to life, Caroline thought a little nervously, he would only have to bend his mammoth neck, snap his jaws, and in one bite he could consume a whole Scout troop.

"Boo!"

Caroline jumped and dropped her pencil.

"Sorry, Caroline," said the man behind her. "I didn't mean to scare you, really."

Caroline smiled sheepishly. "That's okay, Mr. Keretsky. You just startled me. How are you?"

Gregor Keretsky was Caroline's hero. Stacy had two heroes: Woodward and Bernstein, the journalists who had broken the Watergate story in the *Washington Post.* And J.P.'s hero was Guglielmo Marconi, the Italian electrical engineer who had invented the wireless receiver. Caroline could drive her brother into a screaming rage whenever she wanted to, just by referring to Goo-Goo Macaroni.

But she did that only when she was driven to desperation, because she knew how sacred people's heroes were. She was lucky that her hero was right here, in the Museum of Natural History, and that he was one of her best friends. Gregor Keretsky was a vertebrate paleontologist, one of the world's experts on dinosaurs. His office was on the fourth floor of the museum, and sometimes he invited Caroline to have a cup of tea with him. She loved his office; it had bookcases filled with every book that had ever been written about dinosaurs, and some of them had been written by Gregor Keretsky himself.

"I'm fine" — her hero grinned — "and I've been looking for you. I knew my little paleontologist friend would be here, because it is Saturday. And I need your help once again, Caroline."

Caroline sighed. Poor Mr. Keretsky. He had this problem that she helped him with from time to time.

"Neckties?" she asked.

He nodded, embarrassed. "Tomorrow I fly to London. There is a conference there on Monday morning."

"Let's take a look," said Caroline, and she followed him to his office.

He closed the door, because this was a very private consultation. Then he took a Brooks Brothers bag out of a desk drawer. He took three neckties out of the bag and laid them on the top of the desk.

"What do you think?" he asked helplessly.

Poor Mr. Keretsky was colorblind. No one knew, not even his secretary. And he had no wife. Caroline was the only person in the world to whom he had confided his secret problem since 1946. In 1946, when he had left Europe and come to live in the

United States, the Department of Motor Vehicles had refused him a driver's license because he couldn't tell a red light from a green.

His suits were all gray, and his shirts were all white. So those were not a problem. But neckties, he said, made him crazy. He desperately needed help with neckties.

"These two," said Caroline decisively after looking them over. "Keep these two. But take this one back." She wrinkled her nose and handed him the third tie. "It's purple and brown. Really ugly, Mr. Keretsky. Very severely ugly."

"Are you sure?" he asked sadly. "I do like the pattern on this one. It has a—what would you say?—a pleasant geometric order to it."

"Nope," said Caroline firmly. "Take it back."

"The woman at the store said that it was very, very attractive," Mr. Keretsky pointed out.

"What did it cost?"

He turned it over and looked at the price tag. "Twenty-two fifty," he said.

Caroline groaned. "No *wonder* she said it was

very, very attractive. She conned you, Mr. Keretsky. She sold you the ugliest necktie in New York City, for a ridiculously high price. Don't trust her again, under any circumstances."

"All right," he said, sighing, and put the tie back into the bag. "But the others, they are not ugly? You are certain?"

"The others are fine. The striped one's gray and dark green, with a little yellow. And the paisley's some nice shades of blue. They'll look nice on you."

"Caroline," said Gregor Keretsky, "you have once again preserved my dignity. Come to the cafeteria with me and I will buy you a big ice cream."

Caroline fingered her notebook. She really didn't want to miss a chance to talk to one of the world's most famous vertebrate paleontologists. But she had planned to work on a drawing of *Tyrannosaurus rex* to keep in her file on Frederick Fiske.

She compromised. "Okay," she said. "I'll go to the cafeteria. But would you do me a favor? Would you tell me everything you know about *Tyrannosaurus rex?*"

Gregor Keretsky began to laugh. "Caroline," he said, "that would take me days, I think!"

She laughed, too. She knew he was right. "Well," she said, "tell me a *little* about him, then, over some ice cream."

"By the way," she whispered, as they waited for the elevator. "I wouldn't wear those cufflinks to London if I were you."

"These?" Mr. Keretsky held up one wrist. "Why not? These I just bought. There is something wrong with them?"

"Mr. Keretsky," Caroline said as tactfully as she could, "they're *pink*."

"So, Caroline, what would you like to know about old *Tyrannosaurus rex*?" asked Gregor Keretsky, as he put sugar into his coffee. "And why? I think by now, from all the reading you do, that you must know a very great deal already."

Caroline smoothed the top of her ice cream with her spoon. "I'm just doing some general research," she said. "Maybe I'll write a report for school, for science class. So if there's anything I've forgotten, something I might leave out—well, just tell me anything that comes into your mind."

Mr. Keretsky sipped his coffee and wrinkled his forehead into furrows. Caroline was familiar with his way of thinking; she had watched him do it before, and she had watched her brother, J.P., think in the same way. Their brains were like computers.

She watched while Gregor Keretsky fed the topic "*Tyrannosaurus rex*" into his brain, and the computer whirred, picking out bits of information, while his forehead crinkled into ridges. In a minute, she knew, he would open his mouth and the information would come out in an orderly list. She waited. She lapped at a spoonful of ice cream.

"*Tyrannosaurus rex*," he said suddenly, and his brow smoothed, "lived seventy million years ago, in the western part of North America—"

"Des Moines?" asked Caroline, with her mouth full.

But Mr. Keretsky shook his head. "More farther west," he said. "But there was a slightly different form of Tyrannosaurus in Mongolia—"

"No," interrupted Caroline. "Today I'm only

interested in the American version." She figured that Frederick Fiske had probably descended from Americans.

"He weighed about seven and a half tons," Mr. Keretsky went on.

"Not anymore," Caroline murmured. "He's thin, now."

Gregor Keretsky didn't hear her. He was still whirring information from his computer brain to his mouth.

"Twenty feet tall," he said. "That would be—" He looked around the cafeteria and up to the ceiling, measuring the distance with his eyes.

"—about three basketball players standing on top of each other," Caroline suggested.

Mr. Keretsky's computer shut down. He laughed and looked at her in surprise. "It would?" he asked. "Never before have I thought of that analogy. I do not know basketball well. I have seen games, of course, on television, but somehow they have no enjoyment for me." Suddenly he looked downcast. He sipped his coffee again.

"I know, Mr. Keretsky," said Caroline sympathetically. "I understand."

"I cannot tell who is winning, Caroline," he whispered across the table, "or which player belongs to which team. To me their uniforms are all gray."

Caroline tried very hard to think of something comforting to say to someone who could see only gray. "Mr. Keretsky," she said, "just think how much you're able to enjoy elephants!"

He nodded grudgingly. "That is true," he acknowledged. "I do enjoy elephants." But he continued to look mournful.

"Also, your hair is gray," Caroline pointed out. "It's really a very nice color."

Gregor Keretsky smoothed his hair with one hand. "Is it?" he asked, blushing. "Thank you, Caroline. You cheer me up always."

Caroline ate the last melted bits of ice cream in her bowl and leaned forward. "Mr. Keretsky," she asked in a serious voice, "do you think it's possible that there might still be some dinosaurs like *Tyrannosaurus rex* around?"

"Caroline, my little paleontologist," Gregor Keretsky scolded her, "you should know the answer to that question. You have only to look at the alligator. The great Galápagos tortoise. The iguana. Even my friend the elephant—"

"I didn't mean them, exactly." Caroline stopped to think for a second. What she meant, actually, was a little hard to explain. "I mean something that has evolved so that it seems almost human. So that if it was wearing, say, a business suit, you wouldn't be able to tell it from a lawyer or a college professor."

Gregor Keretsky drained the last of his coffee, laughing. He hadn't taken her seriously. "Caroline," he said with a chuckle, "these lawyers, these professors. They all look alike in their—what did you call them?—business suits. But I think they are not dinosaurs, certainly."

"Right." She smiled, and decided to change the subject. It was too soon to introduce the Tate Theory to Gregor Keretsky. She would have to wait until she had more proof.

"I gotta go," she said, standing up and pushing

back her chair. "Have a good time in London. I'll see you when you get back."

Gregor Keretsky smiled. "See you later, alligator," he said.

"After while, crocodile," Caroline responded.

It was a silly way to say goodbye. But it seemed very meaningful, between vertebrate paleontologists.

SIX

ON MONDAY MORNING CAROLINE threw some overnight things into her gym bag. Everyone had agreed that it would be easier if she spent the night at Stacy's instead of coming home across New York City after dinner. Stacy's parents didn't mind. They never minded. Into the top of the bag, she thrust something she had bought, on Saturday, for Stacy. She grinned as she wedged it in on top of the pajamas, poking it down between two furry bedroom slippers.

"Bye, Steg," she said, as she returned her stuffed

Stegosaurus to his hiding place on the closet shelf. No way would she take a stuffed animal to Stacy's overnight. Some things you don't tell even your best friend.

The apartment was quiet. J.P. had already left for school; he refused to be seen riding the bus or walking on a public street with his sister.

And her mother had left already for work. Most mornings she was still there when Caroline and J.P. ate their breakfast. But this morning she had gotten up at five a.m. She hadn't intended to. But it had something to do with her clock radio, which J.P. had returned to her after a weekend of fooling with its insides. Caroline had heard bits and pieces through her closed bedroom door, very early, when it was still dark outside.

"James Priestly Tate, Jr.!" she had heard her mother roar.

After a moment she had heard a groggy response from her brother.

"Would you please explain to me," said Joanna Tate angrily, "why, although I set this alarm for seven a.m., it is still pitch dark outside? What time is it, anyway?"

Caroline could hear the click of a lamp being turned on. A crack of light appeared under her door. She pulled the sheet over her head and listened sleepily.

"It's five oh four," muttered J.P. Caroline could picture him looking at his digital watch with half-open eyes.

"Wake up and look at this clock, J.P.," demanded her mother. "Just look! It says eleven twenty-two. The alarm is set for seven, the clock says eleven twenty-two, and you tell me it's actually five oh four. What have you done to my clock?"

"Lemme see," said J.P. There was a long silence.

"That's weird," Caroline could hear her brother say.

"What's weird?" her mother asked.

"Look at the calendar part," J.P. said. His voice was wide awake now. Caroline could tell that he was becoming interested in the mystery of the clock radio. She could tell that her mother was not.

"That calendar is irrelevant," Joanna Tate said, still angry. "I know what *day* it is. It's Monday, April third. What I want to know is why—"

"But look, Mom," insisted J.P. "Where it says the date? It says February 19, 1997! I must have screwed that up somehow! I've entered a Time Warp!"

"The only thing you are going to enter is Des Moines, Iowa, by bus, if you don't fix my clock radio," said his mother icily.

Caroline hugged Stegosaurus and drifted back to sleep. When she woke up, her mother had left early for work, and Beastly was headed out the door. The clock radio sat on the coffee table, its back removed. Caroline looked at her own Timex; it was seven forty-five.

"Why didn't you wake me up, you turkey? I don't even have time to eat breakfast!"

J.P. smiled pleasantly at her and closed the door noisily behind him, without saying goodbye. Caroline threw one of her bedroom slippers at the closed door. Then she picked it up and hurried to pack her bag.

Before she left the apartment, she wrote a note to her mother and left it on the kitchen table.

Dear Mom:
   Be sure to eat those THINGS for dinner tonight. I don't want to come home if they are still in the house.
   Love,
   Caroline

She couldn't bring herself to write the word *parsnips.*

"I'm so glad you're spending the night tonight," said Stacy happily as they walked beside the park, up Fifth Avenue, after school. Spring was really here. Birds were singing and chirping, and both girls were wearing sweaters, finally, after a long winter of down jackets. "We have so much to do!"

"Yeah," said Caroline gloomily. "Like the math homework."

Caroline couldn't understand fractions. Fractions

didn't make any sense to Caroline *at all,* and her arithmetic book felt like a huge and horrible weight in her backpack. She could almost feel the list of problems on page 43, stabbing her between the shoulder blades.

"That math's not due till Wednesday," said Stacy. "Get your mom to help you with it. She'll know how to do fractions. People who work in banks have to be good at math."

"Wrong," said Caroline. "My mom says they only do decimals in banks."

"Caroline," Stacy pointed out patiently, "Miss Wright said just today, in class, that we have to master fractions because next year we get decimals. And we can't do decimals until—"

"Right," said Caroline, making a face. "Until we've mastered fractions. So?"

"So. Your mother must have mastered fractions. Because now she works at a bank, where they do decimals. She'll be able to help you."

"Maybe." Stacy was probably right, Caroline realized. The weight of the arithmetic book seemed to lighten a bit.

"Anyway, we have lots of other stuff to do, besides homework, tonight. Did you bring that note? The one to the killer from the secret agent?"

Caroline nodded. She had the sinister note to Frederick Fiske tucked inside one of her bedroom slippers.

"We have to analyze that some more," Stacy went on. "There may be clues that we missed. You know, when you're an investigative reporter, like I am, you learn to notice clues everywhere. For example—" Stacy stopped short suddenly. Her forehead wrinkled under her neatly trimmed dark bangs. "Did you notice *that?*"

Caroline looked around. A woman was wheeling a baby carriage through the entrance to the park. A taxi had pulled over to the curb to pick up a passenger. Two pigeons were waddling on the sidewalk. A jogger had just passed. Nothing seemed out of the ordinary.

"What?" she asked.

Stacy was frowning. "The jogger was an impostor. A fake jogger."

Caroline glanced back. The jogger was continuing on, panting and perspiring. He had hairy legs. He looked just like a million other joggers.

"What do you mean?" she asked. "That's not fake sweat. I could smell it when he went past."

"You're not a trained observer like me," said Stacy. "He has a pack of Marlboros in the pocket of his shirt. No *real* jogger smokes Marlboros. It's a dead giveaway." She sighed. "Probably I should make a note of it in my investigative notebook. He could be an escaped criminal or something. But honestly, Caroline, one human being can only do so much. And right now I'm concentrating on Harrison Ledyard. Remember that ripped bra in his trash? The man could well be a crazed killer. Tonight we'll have to—"

"Stacy," Caroline interrupted. "That reminds me. I brought you something. Come over here for a minute and I'll get it out of my bag."

They entered the park, sat down on a bench, and Caroline dug into her gym bag, between the bedroom slippers.

"Here," she said, handing it to Stacy. "You owe

me a dollar twenty-five. I wouldn't ask you, except your allowance is so much bigger than mine."

Stacy took it between two fingers and eyed it with disdain. "A *People* magazine? Caroline Tate! What on earth? Don't tell me you have a crush on some rock star or something! Caroline, my interests go far, far beyond the world of shallow glamour and tasteless gossip. *Honestly!*" She dangled the magazine from her fingers without looking at it. "Here. Take it back. If you think I'm going to pay you a dollar twenty-five for something I could read in my orthodontist's waiting room—"

Caroline grinned smugly. "Turn to page sixty-eight," she said.

Stacy looked at her suspiciously. Then she opened the magazine and found page 68. Her shoulders stiffened. "What the—" she exploded. Then she read, silently, for a minute. "Who wrote this? How did they find all this stuff out? That's not fair! For a *month* I've been up to my elbows in that guy's trash—I mean cigarette butts and old carbon paper, Caroline. I've been doing the nitty-gritty work of investigation! And then some pipsqueak reporter comes along and steals my story! What ever happened to journalistic ethics? Who *wrote* this? There's not even a name on it!"

She flipped angrily through the pages, and then back to 68. Caroline leaned over her shoulder and read the headline again, PULITZER WINNER TAKES ANOTHER PRIZE. In smaller print, underneath, it said, "Acclaimed Author Harrison Ledyard Claims Hometown Sweetheart As Bride." Photographs showed the chubby, balding man grinning as he and his wife vacuumed their apartment together and washed the dishes, wearing matching aprons.

"Come on," said Stacy furiously. She stood up and began walking out of the park. "I'm going to get to the bottom of this."

"Bottom of what?" asked Caroline, running to catch up. "He got married, that's all. And his wife threw away an old bra. Bottom of *what?*"

Stacy slapped the magazine back and forth between her hands as she walked. "I'm going to find out how *People* magazine scooped me on a blockbusting story I've been investigating for weeks!"

"What are you going to do?"

Stacy sighed. "I *could* hang around the Time-Life Building, I suppose, and search their trash for clues. But that might take weeks. Anyway, they probably shred their evidence. I think this particular problem calls for a direct, aggressive approach." She groaned. "I *hate* the direct, aggressive approach. You don't get to wear a disguise or anything. But at least I can use one of my fake voices."

"How?" They were approaching Stacy's apartment building. "How are you going to use a fake voice?" Caroline asked, hurrying to catch up with Stacy at the front door.

"Good afternoon, Mr. Santos," said Stacy, tossing her hair back and speaking in a cool, poised voice to the doorman. "Isn't this spring weather lovely?"

In the elevator, she turned to Caroline and asked, "What did you think of my voice to Mr. Santos?"

Caroline shrugged. "It was okay, I guess. But you sounded about forty years old."

"Right. Good. That's the effect I want. I'm going to use that voice when I call *People* magazine and inquire about their investigative methods."

· · ·

Caroline sprawled on one of the beds in Stacy's room and looked around. Sometimes she really wished her family were rich. Stacy had her own TV. She had her own typewriter, which sat on a polished desk with a matching chair. Everything in the room matched. The wallpaper, pale yellow with pink and green flowers, matched the dust ruffles on the two beds, which matched the draperies and even the lampshades. The only jarring notes were Stacy's backpack, which she had dropped on the floor in the middle of the green carpeting, and her sweater, which she had draped over a lamp.

Even her telephone, on the table between the two beds, was pale yellow. Stacy was sitting cross-legged on her own bed, writing down the number she had found in the telephone directory. Finally she looked up, took a few deep breaths, and dialed.

"Good afternoon," she said in her fake mature voice. "This is Ms. Baurichter. I'm with Bentley, Baurichter, and Bernstein, Attorneys? I would like to inquire as to whom—ah, what I mean is, I want to know who wrote the article about Harrison Ledyard in this week's issue."

She pressed her hand over the receiver and whispered to Caroline, "They're checking."

"Thank you so much," she said, returning to the telephone. "Is he in, by any chance?"

"They're transferring my call," she whispered. "Michael Small. That's his name. What an *ordinary* name. Boy, when *I'm* doing investigative reporting for a national magazine, I'm going to change my — Hello? Mr. Small?

"Mr. Small, I'm calling you to inquire about your methods for obtaining the material for an article such as the one on Harrison Ledyard. It's a *brilliant* piece of reporting, by the way."

She covered the receiver and grinned at Caroline. "Flattery is a very effective way of getting information," she whispered.

Caroline could hear a man's voice on the telephone. She couldn't hear what he was saying, but Stacy was listening intently.

"Yes," said Stacy. "Oh, I see. Yes. Of course. Mr.

Small, didn't you have to do any undercover-type work? I mean, you didn't consider looking through his trash cans or anything?"

Caroline could hear the man laugh. He went on talking.

"Oh," said Stacy, when he had finished. "I would certainly like to congratulate you on a fine job, Mr. Small."

"What?" Caroline could hear that the man was asking a question. "Mr. Small," said Stacy angrily, in her own voice, forgetting to use the fake one, "I wasn't rude enough to ask you how old *you* are. It's none of your business how old I am."

She listened as the man said something else. "Well," she said finally, "thank you for your interest. And for the information. Goodbye."

She hung up. She sat there glumly for a minute as Caroline watched; then she threw the telephone book across the room. It landed on the floor next to her backpack.

"Shoot," she said.

"What's the matter?" asked Caroline. "What did he say?"

"He *said*," said Stacy in an irritated voice, "that I should work on my school newspaper; that it's a good way to start to get experience in journalism. How did he know I was still in school? Didn't I sound mature?"

"I thought you did," acknowledged Caroline. "What else did he say? About Harrison Ledyard?"

Stacy groaned and flopped back on her pillow with her hands behind her head.

"He simply called up Harrison Ledyard and arranged an interview. Of all the dumb ways to go about investigative reporting. He went there for a day. He even took a photographer with him. What if the man had been a crazed murderer?" She sat back up and looked at Caroline. "What was his name—Michael Small? What a *dope*. He could have found himself, unarmed, right in the apartment of a brutal killer. Now if he had gone about it the way he should have, sifting through trash, doing surveillance work—"

"Stacy," suggested Caroline tentatively, "I think you're mixing up detective work and magazine work. I mean, *maybe* you are."

"Well," sighed Stacy. "The heck with Harrison Ledyard. Let him stay up there and vacuum with his hometown sweetheart. At least we have another case to work on. At least we know that other guy's a crazed killer. What was his name?"

"Frederick Fiske."

"And now at least we have some new ideas for methods, from Michael Small. We might consider calling for an interview and taking a photographer."

Caroline shuddered. "I don't think so, Stace. This guy isn't just a killer. He's a *child* killer. And you and me, Stacy, after all, we're—"

"Oh, Caroline," groaned Stacy. "I know. We're children. Don't remind me, please. Michael Small already brought it to my attention in a very tactless way."

There was a knock on the bedroom door. Caroline and Stacy both jumped. "Stand over there, Caroline," hissed Stacy under her breath, "by the closet door. I'll be here behind this chair. If they have weapons—"

The door opened. "Girls," said Mrs. Baurichter, looking in, "dinner's almost ready."

SEVEN

CAROLINE LOVED HAVING DINNER at the Baurichters'. She had eaten there before, and it was always wonderful — not just the food, although the food was always wonderful, but the whole atmosphere. The huge dining room, with deep gray walls and draperies; the crystal chandelier sparkling above the table; the tablecloth — tonight it was pale blue — and the silver candlesticks, with blue candles glowing and dripping wax slowly down their slender sides. At the ends of the table, at Stacy's parents' places, white wine stood in half-filled stemmed glasses.

Once Caroline had asked Stacy why the wineglasses were always only half full, and Stacy had explained that that was the correct way to serve wine. Caroline planned to remember that the entire rest of her life so that she would never do it wrong.

At her own place, as well as Stacy's, across the table, there was a tall glass of ice-cold milk.

It was so different, Caroline thought, from her own house, where they ate dinner at the kitchen table because they had no dining room. J.P. always bolted his food with disgusting manners, because he was always in a hurry to get back to some project in his room. And Joanna Tate, Caroline's mother, was always tired and apologetic. Tired from work. Apologetic for the food.

"What's this?" Caroline had asked one night, poking suspiciously at a casserole.

"It's called Seafood Surprise," said her mother.

That sounded okay. Caroline spooned a big helping onto her plate. "What's the surprise?" she asked. "Why is it called Seafood Surprise?"

"Well, ah," her mother answered, beginning to sound apologetic, "it's because when you think 'seafood' you probably think of shrimp, lobster, scallops, right?"

"Right," said Caroline, with a forkful halfway to
her mouth.

"Well, surprise!" said Joanna Tate. "It's all tuna
fish!"

"Oh," said Caroline sadly. By then she could tell
it was all tuna fish. It was in her mouth.

"I'm sorry," said her mother.

"It's okay," Caroline had said. "Tuna fish isn't
that bad."

At the Baurichters', nothing would ever be
called "Surprise." From the kitchen door, the maid
appeared with a tray, and carefully she placed a
shrimp cocktail at each place.

I have died, thought Caroline, and gone to
heaven. Shrimp cocktail. Even when her family went
to dinner in a restaurant, which they did now and
then for a special occasion, she could never order
shrimp cocktail, because it always cost something
like six dollars. She was allowed to order it only if
she didn't have a main course.

Happily she speared her first shrimp, after

waiting to be certain that Mrs. Baurichter had picked up her fork. Heaven.

"Tate," said Mr. Baurichter suddenly.

"What?" said Caroline with her mouth full. It was startling, to be called "Tate" by Stacy's father, who was wearing a three-piece suit and looked very distinguished. Sometimes Stacy called her "Tate," or some of her other friends, yelling across the school grounds: "Hey, Tate! Wait up!"

"Tate," he said again. Apparently he was only thinking about the name. "I don't think we know any Tates, do we, Helen?"

"I can't recall any," murmured Mrs. Baurichter.

"Of course there's the Tate Gallery," Mr. Baurichter said, wiping his mouth with the pale blue napkin. "Does your family have any connection with the Tate Gallery, in London, Caroline?"

"I don't think so," said Caroline.

"Did Stacy tell me you live on the West Side?"

"Yes. I take the crosstown bus to school," said Caroline politely.

Mrs. Baurichter wiped her mouth and placed her knife and fork on her plate. Caroline couldn't believe it. She had eaten only two shrimp. She was *leaving* shrimp uneaten. "You're fortunate to live on the West Side," said Mrs. Baurichter. "Many creative people live over there. Musicians, writers; I imagine you have many fascinating neighbors."

"A violin player lives in my building," Caroline told her.

"Really?" asked Mrs. Baurichter with interest. "Whom does he play with?"

Panic. Caroline thought as hard as she could about Mr. DeVito. As far as she knew, he was the only violin player at the Little Hungary Cafe.

"He's a soloist," she said finally.

"No one will ever measure up to Oistrakh," said Mr. Baurichter firmly. "At least not in the Sibelius Concerto."

"Well, it's all a matter of preference," said Mrs. Baurichter. "What does your father do, Caroline?"

"Well, ah, he's in sporting goods," Caroline said, and ate another shrimp.

"That's interesting," said Stacy's father. "I play a lot of squash, myself. Does your father—"

"He lives in Des Moines," Caroline explained

hastily. "My parents are divorced, and I live with my mother. My mother works in a bank."

The maid came in and took away the shrimp plates. Caroline was the only one who had eaten all of her shrimp. Sadly she watched the uneaten shrimp disappear, heading for the kitchen. She hoped the maid would get to eat them.

Mr. Baurichter stood up, picked up the wine bottle, and added wine to his wife's glass and then his own. He made them just half full again.

"I find it remarkable," he said, "how many women are entering banking these days. It used to be a male-dominated profession, like law and medicine. Now the vice president of my bank is a woman, and—"

"Mr. Baurichter," interrupted Caroline. Even though she knew it was rude to interrupt, she wanted to set the record straight. "My mother's only a bank teller. She's not really what you would call a *banker*."

"Caroline's family doesn't have much money," Stacy explained matter-of-factly. "She and her brother both have full scholarships at school. And they're practically the smartest kids in the whole school, even though Caroline's lousy at math."

"Well, good for you, Caroline!" said Mr. Baurichter. "Tell me, do you have any idea what you want to be when you grow up?"

Most kids hated it when grownups asked that. But Caroline didn't mind. It sounded as if Mr. Baurichter was really interested.

"Yes," she said proudly. "I'm going to be a vertebrate paleontologist."

"Kid Digs Paleolithic Age," headlined Stacy.

"Actually," explained Caroline politely, "it's the Mesozoic Era that interests me most."

The maid brought in plates of steak. Sizzling, juicy, thick. Paradise, thought Caroline.

"Goodness," said Mrs. Baurichter, "you certainly live in the perfect place, then, over near the Museum of Natural History."

"Yes." Caroline grinned and picked up her steak knife. "I spend a lot of time there."

"You know," said Stacy suddenly, "even though you said all those creative people live on the West

Side, we have a writer here in our own building. Harrison Ledyard."

Mrs. Baurichter groaned; a tasteful, quiet sort of groan.

"That man," she said, "is a complete bore."

The maid had appeared again and was coming around to each place. She was putting something down in front of each person. It was something weird. Caroline watched. Maybe it was some strange sort of decoration. Each one was a huge, fat, gray-green *thing* with what looked like leaves all over it. Looking out of the corner of her eye, Caroline saw that each of them — Mr. Baurichter, Mrs. Baurichter, and Stacy — was reaching for the thing. With their *fingers*.

"What do you mean, a bore?" asked Stacy. "I didn't even know you knew him."

"We went to a cocktail party at his apartment last week," her mother explained. Caroline watched in amazement as she removed a piece of the giant gray-green object, dipped it into a sauce, and then — yes — actually put it into her mouth. Stacy was doing the same thing. She was doing it as if it were no big deal; as if it were a casual, everyday event to *eat* a huge, gross, leafy *thing*.

Mrs. Baurichter went on. "He had a party to celebrate his marriage. So we went and met his new wife, who was actually rather charming—though somewhat out of her element, I think. She's from the Midwest. I'm sorry, Caroline, I know you said your father lives in Des Moines. I didn't mean to disparage the Midwest."

Caroline wasn't even listening. She chewed her steak slowly, watching them actually *eat* those nauseating things. And hers was still sitting there in front of her. She focused all her mental powers on it, willing it to disappear. But it stayed right there.

"But *he* is a crashing, colossal bore. Wouldn't you say so, Paul?"

Mr. Baurichter nodded his head in agreement. Caroline glanced at Stacy. Stacy had stopped eating altogether. No wonder, thought Caroline. She finally came to her senses and realized that she had been chewing on a repulsive *object*.

"We had to listen to him tell all about his work, which, frankly, was terribly dull, and then he told all about his courtship of this woman, which lasted, apparently, for years. He monopolized every bit of conversation at the party. I suppose we'll have to invite them here sometime, but—" Mrs. Baurichter continued to talk about Harrison Ledyard. Stacy was glowering.

Suddenly Caroline realized why. All those hours Stacy had spent wallowing through Ledyard's trash. She could simply have asked her parents; they *knew* Harrison Ledyard. They could have told her all about him. Poor Stacy. Life as an investigative reporter was filled with hazards and frustrations.

Finally Stacy shrugged and began to eat some more of the big round gray-green thing. Caroline looked at hers again. She looked away. She took another bite of steak.

"Hey, Caroline," said Stacy, "if you're too full to eat your artichoke, can I have it? I *love* artichokes."

Caroline smiled politely and passed the disgusting thing across the table to Stacy. Artichoke. So that's what it was called. She hoped her mother never discovered that they existed.

• • •

Later, after they had done their homework and gotten into their pajamas, Caroline and Stacy were lying on the beds in Stacy's room again. Miraculously, during dinner, a maid had come in and picked up Stacy's sweater, folded it, and put it into a drawer. Her backpack had been placed on her desk.

"Sometimes I really wish I were rich," said Caroline, staring at the ceiling. "But if I were rich, maybe I wouldn't ever have the motivation to be a vertebrate paleontologist. Maybe I would go to Asia Minor, and instead of digging in the desert, I would just want to stay in a Hilton Hotel. I wouldn't want that to happen."

"It wouldn't," Stacy answered. "Because look at me for Living Proof. My family's pretty rich—so I guess that makes *me* rich—but I still plan to work very hard. I *already* work hard at being an investigative journalist." She giggled. "Even if I go about it wrong, sometimes. Harrison Ledyard—what a bogus adventure *that* was! Me down there in his trash cans looking for clues, for heaven's sake, and the whole time he was upstairs practically sending out newsletters!"

"You know," said Caroline, "even if he's a colossal bore, like your folks said, I sort of wish that my mother had met him. There he was, an eligible bachelor, and my mother didn't even meet him. My mother never seems to meet any eligible men."

"Caroline," said Stacy in a solemn voice, "I am very worried about your mother."

"Oh, Stace, you don't need to *worry* about her. We're not headed for the poorhouse or anything. And she's not even miserably unhappy. It's just that she never gets to go out on dates or anything. Right at this very moment she's sitting at home, probably doing a crossword puzzle."

"That's why I'm worried. She's sitting at home —alone, except for J.P. —"

"Who is useless. He'll be in his bedroom, inventing something. He doesn't even play Scrabble."

"I'm not talking about games and entertainment and conversation, Caroline," said Stacy, who was sitting up now, talking in a low, hushed voice. "I'm talking about what might also be sitting alone, upstairs, *above* your mother." She paused dramatically.

"The Great Killer." Now Caroline sat up, too. "Frederick Fiske."

"Right. I'm sure he's there in his apartment at this very minute. Friends describe him as a loner, I'm absolutely sure of it."

"Stacy, can I use your phone?"

Caroline dialed the number of her apartment. When her mother answered, she said, "Mom, are you okay?"

"Sure." Her mother laughed. "I'm watching a dumb TV show and painting my fingernails, just for fun. I'll have to take the polish off, because they don't allow it at the bank, but it's kind of fun to try it out. How about you, Caroline? Are *you* okay? You're not homesick, are you?"

"I'm fine, Mom," Caroline said impatiently. "It's you I'm wondering about. How's the building? Is everyone in the building home tonight?"

"Caroline," her mother said, and laughed again, "I haven't made an exhaustive study of that, the way you would. Let me see. Vinnie DeVito's at the Little Hungary, of course, because he never gets home till midnight. But Billy and his mother are home; I saw them coming in from the park about five-thirty."

"I wasn't really thinking of the DeVitos. How about—well, how about the other people in the building, Mom?"

"Nobody home on the second floor. Did I tell you that Miss Edmond is in the hospital? Nothing serious, though; she had some minor surgery, and she'll be home next week. I sent her a card and signed all our names."

Miss Edmond was the retired schoolteacher who lived alone on the second floor.

"Who else, Mom?" asked Caroline tensely.

Her mother said lightly, "The Carrutherses are definitely home. I can hear them. They're chasing each other around the apartment again."

Jason and Nell Carruthers were newlyweds who had recently moved into the fourth floor. Caroline liked them. Nell Carruthers was an actress who sometimes made TV commercials; she was very glamorous on TV, where she used a hair conditioner and then cantered on a horse along a sunny beach.

But in real life she wore jeans all the time, and her hair in a long pigtail. Her new husband was lighting director for a theater. They ran around their apartment, laughing and shrieking very noisily in the evenings, playing tag or something.

"And, ah, what about the fifth floor, Mom?" Caroline asked nervously.

"Fred Fiske? I don't know if he's home or not. I haven't seen him this evening. Why on earth are you interested, Caroline?"

"Stacy and I were watching TV," Caroline lied, "and they said that there was a burglar loose in the city. So I was worried."

Her mother hooted with laughter. "Caroline, there are a *thousand* burglars loose in New York City. You know that as well as I do. Remember J.P. had his lunch money stolen just last week? And by a little old lady? That was the weirdest thing, a little old lady—"

"Mom, be sure to lock all the locks on the door, okay?"

"I always lock all the locks, Caroline. You know that. Relax. Did you do your homework?"

"And the windows, Mom. Be sure to lock the windows."

"Homework, Caroline. Did you do your homework?"

Caroline sighed. "Yes," she said. "Bye, Mom."

She hung up the phone and looked at Stacy. Stacy had unfolded the letter to Frederick Fiske for the hundredth time and was reading it once more, holding it close to the lamp between the beds.

"I think this is typed on a Smith-Corona typewriter," Stacy said, frowning. "What did your mom say?"

Caroline twisted her hair and then wound a strand around one ear. She chewed her lower lip. "It's very bad," she announced.

"What is? What's very bad? What did she say?"

"She called him 'Fred.' Not 'Mr. Fiske.' Not 'the guy on the fifth floor.' But 'Fred.' You realize what this means, Stacy."

"Right. It's bad," muttered Stacy, turning the letter over and over in her hands.

"She's met him. She *knows* him. She's in danger." Stacy corrected her. "No, she isn't. You're forgetting what the letter says, Caroline. It doesn't say, 'Eliminate the woman.' It says, 'The woman's terrific.'"

"That's true, too," said Caroline miserably. "She is. My mother's terrific."

"It's the kids he's after. It says so right here. 'Eliminate the kids.' I'm pretty sure it's a Smith-Corona typewriter."

Stacy got into bed and turned off the lamp.

Caroline climbed under the covers and wrapped her arms around the pillow. She wished suddenly that she had brought her Stegosaurus. But not even a Stegosaurus was a match for *Tyrannosaurus rex*, the Great Killer. "That's *me* he's talking about when he says 'the kids,'" she whispered. "I'm sure of it. Me and J.P."

"Slare stoxtox," mumbled Stacy sleepily from the other bed.

"What?" Caroline lifted her head and peered through the dark.

"SLAYER STALKS TOTS," Stacy repeated. "Good night, Caroline."

Eight

CAROLINE DREAMED. SHE DREAMED the same dream three nights in a row: first when she was sleeping at Stacy's, and then again for two nights in her own bedroom, curled up with her soft Stegosaurus beside her again.

In the dream she was walking barefoot through thick foliage, in a warm, moist jungle where huge trees grew up out of mossy earth. Ferns and vines brushed against her face and arms as she made her way through the tangled undergrowth. Narrow beams of sunlight filtered down through the high branches; all around was the noise of birds calling in shrill cries, and the jungle floor was alive with small creatures scurrying and darting here and there.

She felt very happy in the dream. She knelt, pushing aside thick leaves, and watched some tiny creatures playing. One smiled at her, and she could see its tiny teeth. It wagged its long, thin, scaly tail; she recognized it as a Compsognathus, the very smallest of the dinosaurs. With one finger she stroked its bobbing, three-inch head, and it scampered away to join its timid friends.

Looking up, she watched the flying creatures soaring among the thick trunks of the tall trees. There was the small Pterodactyl, its leathery wings outstretched as it moved from tree to tree, perching now and then on branches and nodding down to her. Much more clumsily, the awkward Archaeopteryx swooped by. She laughed.

Poor Archaeopteryx. It didn't really know whether it was a bird or a lizard. Its feathery wings propelled it from tree to tree, but its long snaky tail was in the way; again and again it lighted on branches, holding tight with the little clawed hands

on the end of each wing, cocked its head, and nodded to Caroline below.

Splash! Caroline turned, in her dream, and
looked at the pond behind her, laughing aloud in
delight to see the huge, ridiculous Anatosaurus
poking his duck-billed face out of the water to grin
at her.

"You ought to have a dermatologist take a look
at those warts," Caroline told him politely. But he
grinned again, tossed his bump-covered head, and
splashed off for a swim.

Suddenly the nature of the dream began to
change. The jungle noises became quiet. The silly
Anatosaurus blinked and submerged. Beneath her
feet, the tiny Compsognathus scuttled away to
hide under a bush. The Pterodactyl and its friend,
Archaeopteryx, gave brief cries of alarm and flew
away.

A chill changed the warm, humid air and made
Caroline shiver. The sunlight that found its way
through the foliage disappeared, consumed by a
monstrous shadow that darkened everything. The
earth beneath her feet began to shake. Terrified, she

looked up and saw the Great Killer moving slowly toward her: *Tyrannosaurus rex*, his teeth exposed in an evil smile, his small claws moving in the air high above her head. Casually he ripped small trees and dropped them to the ground as he made his way closer and closer to where she stood.

"Run," Caroline ordered her dream-self. And she did, knowing as she did that it was hopeless, that the monstrous dinosaur could, with one or two lurching moves, catch up. She glanced back over her shoulder as she stumbled through the tree roots. He was closer. Now his face was clearly visible, even so high above her in the jungle growth. It had a small beard and bushy eyebrows. It was Frederick Fiske.

On Monday night and Tuesday night, she had the dream and woke in a panic. On Wednesday night, she had it again. But this time she didn't wake as quickly. This time the Tyrannosaurus with the face of Frederick Fiske was approaching, tearing the jungle growth aside, when something else appeared at her side and said gruffly, "I'll help you."

It was close to human size—about the size of a man, but it was bent over, supporting itself with a lengthy tail. With one of its thin arms, it took her hand and, in the husky voice, reassured her again. "I'm the one who can save you," it said.

Now she woke. This time she was not terrified, but felt calm and safe. The thin, long-tailed creature was the one who could protect her from Frederick Fiske, the Great Killer. But Caroline groaned, sitting there in her bed, watching the early-morning light begin to appear through her window. She recognized, now that she was wide awake, who her protector had been. It was Coelophysis, her least favorite dinosaur, the one with bad posture and a bad temper. It was her brother, J.P.

Dressing slowly, even before her mother's newly repaired clock radio alarm sounded wake-up time, Caroline thought about the dream. Maybe the nasty-tempered Coelophysis had a good side, after all. Maybe her brother did. Maybe she should tell him that a murderer lived upstairs.

But at breakfast, J.P., while slurping his orange juice with his usual gross manners, furrowed his eyebrows and stared at Caroline malevolently over the top of his glass.

"Why are you staring at me in that creepy way?" Caroline asked. It was unnerving.

J.P. gulped the last of his juice and put his glass down. He grinned. "Someday I'm going to invent a pill that can turn eyeballs into lasers. Then you can incinerate someone just by staring at them."

"Why *me?*"

J.P. shrugged. "You're just a test case. A guinea pig."

"James," said his mother, "if you would divert your inventive energy into worthwhile projects, you could be very successful someday."

"Yeah," he replied. "I could be an only child, too, after the eyeball lasers are perfected."

Joanna Tate sighed in exasperation. "It would be *terrible* to be an only child. It would be *lonely.*"

"WRONG," said Caroline and J.P. in unison. They glared at each other with laser-beam glares.

"Listen," said their mother as she stacked the breakfast dishes, "I want you guys to promise me that you won't kill each other tomorrow night. I'm going out, so you'll be alone here. Alone *together.*"

"What do we get for dinner?" asked J.P. "And can I eat in my room?"

"TV dinners," said his mother. "The fried chicken ones. And yes, you may eat in your room if you *promise* not to leave garbage in there. I do *not* want to have to deal with cockroaches."

"If I perfected my laser eyeballs," mused J.P., picking up his schoolbooks, "I could be an exterminator. I could go around staring at cockroaches. Zap! Zap! Gotcha!" He moved his eyes in all directions, staring fixedly at imaginary cockroaches.

"Where are you going tomorrow night?" asked Caroline as she pulled on her sweater.

Her mother grinned. "I have a dinner date," she said. "First time in ages. He's taking me to an Italian restaurant."

"*Who's* taking you?" Caroline asked. But she knew. Somehow she knew the answer.

"Scoot, guys, you're going to be late for school. It's that nice-looking man who moved in upstairs. Fred Fiske."

. . .

I've got to tell someone, Caroline thought, all day during school. Someone. Not just Stacy. Stacy will just write headlines, KIDS' MOM DATES LONER, Stacy will say. WOOS MOM, SLAYS KIDS.

By afternoon it was all she could think about. In history class, she could hear Mr. Winslow droning on and on about the Phoenicians—and ordinarily Caroline *liked* the Phoenicians—but she didn't listen to what he was saying. Who can I tell? she was thinking.

Then she remembered: Mr. Keretsky would be back by now. Gregor Keretsky was the only person she knew who would go to Europe and then come right back home, not even staying around to have dinner in restaurants or to visit castles. His conference in London, he had said, was only for one day. He would be back in his office at the Museum of Natural History by now. She would visit him there after school. She would tell him everything, even how Frederick Fiske looked like a Tyrannosaurus. Gregor Keretsky would understand how sinister that was. She smiled and relaxed, looking up from her desk just in time to see Mr. Winslow peering over his glasses at her with an irritated frown.

"Caroline?" he was saying. "I don't think you've been listening to a single word. Can you tell the class, please, what the eastern and western boundaries of Phoenicia were?"

Caroline grinned. "The Mediterranean Sea on the west," she said. "And the Lebanon Mountains on the east." Hah, she thought. Even though I'm about to be the victim of a savage crime, I still do my homework, Mr. Winslow.

She jogged home from the bus stop, eager to drop off her books, change into jeans, and head for the Museum of Natural History. J.P. wouldn't be around, thank goodness; he always stayed after school on Thursday for Computer Club. Caroline fished her keys out of her backpack, opened the front door, and stopped to take the mail out of the box marked J. TATE.

Typical, she thought. Dentist bill. Bank statement. Child-support check from Des Moines.

Addressed to her, from the museum, were illustrated brochures telling about a whale-watching expedition and a symposium on primates. She read them through carefully, standing there in the first-floor hallway. Too bad: the whale-watching trip was on a weekend, but it cost a lot. The primate symposium was free, but it was on a weekday afternoon, so she'd be in school. She'd have to write thank-you notes explaining why she couldn't come. She always did that, even though Mr. Keretsky had told her it wasn't necessary. But Caroline was afraid they'd quit inviting her if she never came and didn't explain why. Once, in fourth grade, she had invited a girl named Tamara St. John to come and play on Saturday at least four times, and Tamara St. John had never come and hadn't explained why. Finally Mrs. Tate had explained very gently to Caroline that it appeared that Tamara St. John didn't *want* to come and play at her house, so Caroline had quit inviting her. It seemed like the same sort of thing. So she always wrote a polite note to the President of the Board of Trustees of the Museum of Natural

History, explaining why she couldn't attend seminars or lectures or safaris.

If her mother had simply refused to have dinner with Frederick Fiske without an explanation, she thought suddenly, he would quit inviting her, simple as that.

At the foot of the stairs, she glanced at the last piece of mail—and stopped dead in her tracks. It was another letter to Frederick Fiske from Carl Broderick. It had been in the Tate mailbox by mistake.

Sometimes that happened. Sometimes they found in their mailbox notices of chamber music concerts addressed to Mr. DeVito. Sometimes old Miss Edmond found Caroline's museum mailings in her mailbox by mistake. They would simply leave the mistaken mail on the hall table, and the right person would pick it up.

And that, Caroline realized, was what she should do with Frederick Fiske's letter. But she didn't. She looked back at the hall table, a Victorian monstrosity with an ugly vase full of dried flowers on it. Right there, on the dusty top of that table, was where she should put Frederick Fiske's letter.

Instead, she stuck it in between the two notices from the Museum of Natural History and took it upstairs. Ten minutes later, when she bounded back down the stairs and jogged toward Seventy-Ninth Street and the museum, the letter was in the back pocket of her jeans.

NINE

IN ONE WAY, it was a great comfort to be in Gregor Keretsky's office, drinking tea while her dear, dear friend stirred and sipped his coffee. His desk was covered, as always, with papers in messy stacks; on the shelves around the walls were books and bones and small replicas of different kinds of prehistoric mammals. Mr. Kerestsky was tilted back in his leather chair, with his feet up on his desk, the way he usually was. And Caroline, as usual, had found a space on his big lumpy couch by moving aside the piles of books that were always there. It was the coziest place in the whole world, she thought.

But she was frowning and feeling less comfortable than she ordinarily did in that room. Gregor Keretsky hadn't reacted the way she had expected or hoped. The unopened letter to Frederick Fiske lay between them on the corner of his cluttered desk.

"No, Caroline," Mr. Keretsky was saying, for about the third time, "you must not open that letter. It isn't addressed to you. It would be against the law."

"But—"

"No buts. I understand, my little paleontologist. You are frightened of this man."

"He looks like *Tyrannosaurus rex*," Caroline pointed out once more.

"I understand even that. Many of these great beasts take on human qualities for me, too. And Tyrannosaurus—ah, the Great Killer. He is the most horrible of all. He could take you and me together, Caroline, and crush us both in his teeth, and his small brain would have no room in it to feel compassion."

"What if he lived right upstairs from you, Mr. Keretsky?" Caroline asked him.

Gregor Keretsky smiled at her. "It is only a man that lives upstairs, my small scientist. Don't forget that. The world of science must never mix daydreams with reality. These beasts that you and I know so well? They are all in the past. They don't live upstairs, not anywhere. It is a man. It is a man named—what did you tell me?" He leaned forward, his chair squeaking, to peer at the name on the envelope.

"Frederick Fiske," Caroline reminded him.

"Yes. Frederick Fiske. A man's name, that is all. Just as the name Gregor Keretsky is the name of a man, an absentminded man who sees no colors. And the name Caroline Tate, the name of a girl who should maybe be home by now, helping her mama get the dinner ready?" He grinned at her and looked at his watch.

"But, Mr. Keretsky, remember the other letter? The one about getting rid of the kids? And remember, I didn't open that one. It was already open and thrown away."

"Yes, I remember. But there too, Caroline, the daydreams are getting in the way of the thinking. Would a killer—even a killer who looks like the Greatest of Killers—so casually toss away evidence of such a thing? Remember that a man has a *big* brain. This letter you showed to me, surely it has some other meaning. Why did you not show it to your mama?"

"She would have laughed. She would have said that the eighty-third reason she loves me is because I make her laugh so often."

"And is it such a bad thing, to laugh? There is not enough laughter around; that is what I think."

Caroline sighed. She didn't feel at all like laughing. "I thought that if I opened just this one, Mr. Keretsky—"

"No. You must not. In this country it is the law, and one of the most important of laws. A man's mail is his own. It is one of the reasons I came to live in America, Caroline. I have lived in other countries where this could happen, that a man could be accused, his mail opened, false evidence used against him . . ." His voice trailed off, and he gazed through the small office window. "You go home now, Caroline," he said finally, after a long silence. "Come back tomorrow, or maybe Saturday, and I will tell you about the conference in London. I brought you a present, but it is at my apartment because I did not expect to see you today. When you come back, I will tell you about London, and we will eat ice cream together. How would that be?"

Caroline stood and put the letter back into her pocket. "All right," she said. "I'd like to hear about the London conference. And about London. Did you see the Queen's Guards with the red coats?"

"Ah, Caroline." Gregor Keretsky chuckled. "You are teasing me. You know that for me even the coats of the Queen's Guards would be gray. You're the most colorful thing in my life, Caroline, and even then, the color is all here" — he tapped his chest — "in the heart. Never in the eyes. What color are those very practical-looking trousers you are wearing?"

Caroline started to laugh. "Mr. Keretsky," she said, "jeans are always blue."

• • •

Walking slowly back home, Caroline took the sealed letter from her pocket and turned it over and over in her hands. Mr. Keretsky was right, she knew. Once, when she was a little girl and still believed in magic things, she had had a crush on Santa Claus; she had imagined him to be kind and wise and full of fun. Now Gregor Keretsky was all those things — and more, because his past had taught him something about sadness, too. So his wisdom was better wisdom than Santa Claus wisdom. She believed in what he said. And she knew she would not scurry sneakily up to the apartment to turn on the tea kettle and steam the letter open.

But when she held it in front of her to read the address once more, the late-afternoon spring sunlight glinted off a puddle on the sidewalk. Against the light, through the envelope, she could see writing. Almost without looking, she could clearly see the word "poison."

When she entered her building, Caroline guiltily passed the front hall table without putting the letter there. J.P. was home; she could see his jacket and books on the living room couch and could hear him puttering in his room, behind the closed door.

"It's only me," she called so that he wouldn't think a burglar had entered the apartment. He grunted something in reply.

She took the letter into her room and turned on the lamp beside her bed. Carefully she held the unopened letter in front of the bright bulb. And there it was: a short note, typed, and all of it in one place so that it wasn't folded on top of itself. It was the easiest thing in the world to read. It was also the most horrible. Horrible horrible horrible.

Fred:

When this goes through and you get paid, would you install a phone, please?

Have you figured out how to eliminate the children? I know it's tough, but you have to be brutal—and thorough—and quick. The May 1st deadline is inflexible.

About the poisons: I'll leave that to you. But best not to use cyanide, not after the Tylenol thing. Find something obscure.

Carl

Caroline read it twice. Then she read it a third time, slowly, and copied it onto a page of notebook paper. After she was certain she had copied it word for word, with no mistakes, she took the letter back downstairs and deposited it on the table next to the vase of dried flowers.

Trudging back upstairs, she thought again about her dream. It had been, after all, the Coelophysis, ratty-looking though he was, who had come to her rescue, who had said, "I'll help you."

She knocked on her brother's bedroom door and called, "J.P.? Would you come out?"

"Why should I?" he called back.

"Because," said Caroline in despair, "I need your help."

"I have to think, I have to think, I have to think," muttered J.P. nervously, after Caroline had described her suspicions to him and shown him the first note and the copy of the second. "Shut up and let me think."

"How can I shut up when I'm not even saying

anything?" asked Caroline. She went to the kitchen and poured two glasses of orange juice. "Here," she said, handing one to her brother. He was sitting on the living room couch, his elbows on his knees, his chin in his hands.

"I'm thinking. I'm thinking," J.P. repeated, taking the glass of juice absentmindedly. The telephone rang. "Shut the phone up, would you? I'm thinking."

"KID CALLS PAL," announced Stacy over the telephone.

"Hi, Stace," said Caroline. She took the phone into the bathroom so that she wouldn't disrupt J.P.'s thinking process.

"Anything going on? You dashed away after school, and I've been calling and calling, but you weren't home until now."

"Stacy," said Caroline in an ominous voice, "things are getting much more complicated. There was another letter to Frederick Fiske from the secret agent. The murder's got to be before May first because there's a deadline. I've asked J.P. to help. I had to."

"Sibs Foil Crime," said Stacy. "*Sibs* means siblings," she explained. "*Siblings* means brothers and sisters."

"I *know* that," Caroline said patiently. "And right now my sib is figuring out our next move."

"Caroline, this is going to be a big story. I mean a truly big story."

"I know that, Stacy. But I won't be around to read it, not if I've been poisoned."

"No way. You're going to foil it, you and J.P. You foil, I write. This is my big break, Caroline. *Promise* me you won't give it to another journalist."

"Stacy, I don't even *know* another journalist."

"And I'll never divulge my sources, Caroline. If they put me in jail, I won't divulge my sources. That's part of journalistic ethics."

"Stacy," said Caroline, becoming less patient, "you seem to be more interested in your truly big story than you are in your best friend. Don't you realize that I'm the *victim* here?"

"That's *it!*" exclaimed Stacy. "That's my lead! I'm going to write it New Journalism style, and maybe I can sell it to *New York* magazine. Here's the lead,

Caroline; listen to this: 'I met Caroline MacKenzie Tate for the first time when she was eight years old. She beat me in the election for third-grade class secretary, and I called her several names. Smartass. Teacher's pet. I didn't know then what I know now, on this gray, anguished April morning: that Caroline MacKenzie Tate was, when all was said and done, a *victim*.'"

"Stacy Baurichter," said Caroline angrily, "don't you dare use my middle name, not *ever*. And this is not a gray, anguished April morning. This is a sixty-five-degree sunny April afternoon, and it is almost over, and my mother will be home from work in a few minutes, and I am hanging up this phone if you—"

Stacy interrupted her. "Do you think they'll let me say 'smartass'? Censorship is becoming such a problem for us journalists."

Caroline slammed down the telephone receiver before Stacy could do one of her usual headline goodbyes.

Back in the living room, J.P. looked up and stopped muttering. "I've got it," he announced. "I'm going to hot-wire his telephone so that next time he makes a phone call, ZAP!"

"J.P.!" said Caroline. "Would you pay attention, please? I showed you what that letter said. He doesn't even *have* a telephone. He's going to get one after he gets paid for killing us. Too late *then!*"

J.P. frowned. "His toilet seat, then. A few craftily placed wires, and ZAP! Hot-cross buns!"

"Shhh," said Caroline suddenly. They heard the jingling of keys. "Mom's home."

The door opened and Joanna Tate appeared, pulling off her earrings with one hand. "Hi!" she said, cheerfully. "Boy, am I bushed. What are you guys up to? It's the first time in ages that I haven't heard you fighting as I came up the stairs."

Caroline laughed nervously. "Maybe we're finally developing some interests in common," she said.

TEN

"PEEL THE TINFOIL BACK after half an hour so the chicken will get brown, okay?" said Caroline's mother. "And don't forget to lock the door after I leave."

"We always lock the door, Mom," Caroline pointed out.

"How do I look?" Joanna Tate twirled around. "I haven't worn this dress in ages. Does it still fit all right?"

"You look fine," said Caroline glumly. "Doesn't she, J.P.?"

J.P. looked up from his new issue of *Scientific American* and grunted.

"Mom, if you want to stay home, you can have my TV dinner. I'm not very hungry," Caroline said.

"Why would I want to stay home? Did I tell you he's taking me to an Italian restaurant? Spaghetti and Chianti. Yum." She went to the mirror near the front door and combed her hair again.

"I don't like that guy," muttered Caroline.

"Fred Fiske? You don't even know him."

"Neither do you," Caroline said meaningfully.

"I don't know him *well*. But I've been walking to the corner with him lots of mornings. He goes down to get a newspaper at the drugstore by my bus stop."

"You don't even know what he does for a living."

"Well, I know that he's a history professor at Columbia. But he's on a year's leave of absence, because he's got some project."

"Right," said Caroline. "And you don't know what that project *is*."

"True, he's kind of mysterious about that. But when someone says he's working on a project, you don't become overly inquisitive. I don't do that to you, James, do I? When you're working on a project in your room, I don't stand at the door, saying 'Tell me all about your project, James. I want to know all about your project.' I don't, do I, James?"

J.P. turned a page of his magazine and looked up. "No," he acknowledged. "You stand at my door and yell, 'If you're taking the toaster apart again I'm buying you a tourist-class ticket to Des Moines!'"

"Tell you what, Caroline," suggested her mother. "If it turns out that Fred Fiske is taking toasters apart up there in his apartment, I'll never have dinner with him again. Fair enough?"

"You never take me seriously," Caroline muttered.

Her mother came over and kissed the top of her head. She smelled of cologne. "Of course I do. But not when you're being silly. And the thirty-fourth thing I love about you, Caroline, is that you're so silly so often."

Since it was apparent that her mother was not going to change her mind and stay home, Caroline decided to change the subject. "Mom," she said, "I had a fight with Stacy. I hung up on her when we were talking on the phone yesterday. We didn't speak to each other all day, except for once in gym class, and then all she said was, 'Kɪᴅ Sɴᴜʙs Bᴇsᴛ Pᴀʟ.' Can I invite her to come for dinner on Sunday?"

"Sure," said her mother, glancing at her watch. "I have a leg of lamb in the freezer. It'd be fun to have company. We haven't had company for ages."

"Hey," said Caroline suddenly. "Can I invite somebody else, too? I told my friend Mr. Keretsky that I'd invite him for dinner sometime."

"I guess so. But you're not trying to cook up a romance, are you?"

The thought made Caroline giggle in spite of her bad mood. "No," she said. "He's at least seventy years old, I think. Too old even for you."

"Well, sure. Go ahead and invite him. We'll have a real dinner party. Shhhh — did you hear a knock?" There was a second knock on the door. "Be polite. Even if it kills you," she whispered as she went to answer it.

Caroline and J.P. said "How do you do" very

politely to Frederick Fiske. Then their mother was gone in a flurry of smiles and the lingering scent of her cologne. She went down the stairs on the arm of the killer.

Caroline watched through the apartment window until the pair had walked as far as the corner and disappeared from view. J.P. had put his magazine down and was on his feet, pacing.

"How long do you think they'll be gone?" Caroline asked him.

He put on his stern, scientific look and calculated in his head. "Twenty minutes to get to the restaurant. Twenty minutes to eat spaghetti. Twenty minutes to come home. They'll be gone an hour. Five minutes longer if they have dessert."

Caroline sighed. Sometimes, for all his high IQ, her brother was a moron. "J.P.," she pointed out, "this is a *date*. It isn't a speed-eating contest. They won't be home till ten, I bet. Maybe even eleven."

"Well, I don't know what they can do all that time in an Italian restaurant. I could eat *two* orders of spaghetti in twenty minutes. But I hope you're right. That gives me plenty of time." J.P. started looking through the pockets of his corduroy pants.

"What *exactly* are you going to do? No hot wires; remember, you promised while Mom was getting dressed."

Her brother was holding his Swiss Army knife, his bus pass, tweezers, some paper clips, and the tiny screwdriver he used every time he took the toaster apart. "I'm just going to collect evidence. I can get his door open using the knife and the bus pass. I always open our door that way when I lose my keys."

"You'll need gloves so you won't leave finger-prints."

"Right." J.P. went to the closet in the hall, poked around, and came back wearing thick knitted mit-tens. "These won't work," he said in disgust. "They're like *paws.*"

"Here, try these." Caroline brought her moth-er's rubber gloves from under the kitchen sink. J.P. put them on. They were huge and bright turquoise. "Gross," he muttered.

"One more thing," he said. "Get me some envelopes. I'll need them to put the evidence in."

Caroline went to her mother's desk and took out three envelopes. J.P. took them awkwardly in his rubber gloves, folded them, and stuffed them into his back pocket.

"What if you find *big* evidence?" asked Caroline apprehensively. "Those envelopes won't hold much."

"I'll hire a U-Haul trailer," said J.P. sarcastically. He headed for the door. "If you hear them coming back, run up the stairs and warn me."

Caroline nodded. "Do you want a pencil and paper so you can write stuff down?" she asked.

J.P. shot her a withering look. "Don't forget that I have a photographic memory," he said. "I never have to write anything down." Then he was gone.

It was beginning to get dark. Caroline turned on the living room lamps. She went to the kitchen and peeled back the tinfoil from the TV dinners. She glanced out the window again to make sure her mother and Frederick Fiske weren't returning unexpectedly, but there was only a young couple, arms around each other, on the corner, and an old woman trudging along with a large bag of groceries.

She looked up Gregor Keretsky's telephone number in the Manhattan telephone book and called him. She felt a little nervous, because she had never called him at home before; she had never seen him, in fact, outside the Museum of Natural History. But he responded cheerfully, and with a funny formal kind of politeness, that he would be delighted to come for dinner at six on Sunday.

She checked the stove, found that the chicken was brown and sizzling, and turned the oven off.

She opened the apartment door, listened in the hall, and heard nothing. The Carrutherses, upstairs, apparently weren't home. Downstairs, Miss Edmond's apartment was silent as well; she was still in the hospital. On Fridays, Mrs. DeVito usually took Billy to the Little Hungary for dinner, where they got a discount if they ordered the special. Probably no one was home in the entire building except J.P. and Caroline. The silence was scary.

She called Stacy on the phone and apologized for her half of their fight.

"Tiff Ends," announced Stacy. "Thank goodness."

"J.P.'s upstairs, Stacy," whispered Caroline. "He broke into Frederick Fiske's apartment and he's up there now, looking for evidence."

"You should have called me first," Stacy said tersely. "You *know* I'm an expert on evidence. Is he wearing gloves?"

"Yes. Big turquoise rubber ones."

"Good. That's essential, to wear gloves. Is he writing everything down?"

"He doesn't have to. J.P. has a photographic memory. He can memorize a whole list of spelling words just by looking at it for five seconds."

"Ohhh," groaned Stacy. "Is he *lucky*! I'd give anything to have a photographic memory! I wish I knew your brother better, Caroline. He and I could team up and—"

"J.P. is a creep," Caroline said impatiently.

"I think he's kind of cute," Stacy said. "Well,

anyway, no need to have another fight. Listen, does he know that there has to be a corpus delicti?"

"A what?"

"Corpus delicti. All the evidence in the world is no good unless there's a corpus delicti. My father told me that."

"But what *is* it?"

Stacy hesitated a minute. "I forget," she said, finally. "That's why I wish I had a photographic memory. But you have to find one. Tell J.P."

"Okay." Caroline wrote it down, spelling it as well as she could. "I have to go. But listen, the reason I called was to ask if you could come for dinner on Sunday. Six o'clock."

"PAL SAYS YES," said Stacy, and she hung up.

Caroline looked through the window again; the street was empty now. The streetlights had come on. She took the piece of paper on which she had written the incomprehensible words, went out into the hall, listened to the silence again, and then went up two flights of stairs. Frederick Fiske's door was closed. She reached for the doorknob, realized she was not wearing gloves, and finally knocked on the door with the toe of her shoe.

"J.P.?" she called softly through the door. "It's only me."

He opened the door a few inches and peered through the crack. "I'm almost through," he said softly. "What do you want? Are they coming home?"

Caroline shook her head. "No. But I talked to Stacy and she said that evidence is no good unless you find a"—she looked at the paper in the dim hall light—"corpus delicti."

"What's that?"

"I don't know. Neither does Stacy. But she's positive you have to have one."

"Read it again, slowly."

"Corpus delicti." Caroline pronounced the words as precisely as she could.

"It's Latin," J.P. mused. "And I don't take Latin till next year. But I leafed through Mark Peterson's Latin book once. Let me see it, Caroline. A photographic memory only works if you *see* something."

She handed him the paper through the crack in the door, and he took it in his giant gloves.

"Yeah," he said after a moment, and handed the paper back. "Got it. No sweat. We have one."

"What *is* it?"

"I don't know what 'delicti' means. That didn't register anything on my photographic memory. But *corpus* means 'body' in Latin."

"*Body?* BODY?"

"Shhhhhh."

"You found a *body?*" Caroline was trying to be quiet, but she could hear her voice rising shrilly. She backed away from Frederick Fiske's door.

"Yes. Now go back down and stand guard. I'll be down in a minute."

ELEVEN

CAROLINE WAS GNAWING HALFHEARTEDLY on a chicken leg when the apartment door finally opened and J.P. came in, carrying the three envelopes carefully in his gloved hands. She glanced behind him nervously, to the hall, but there was nothing there. For a moment she had been afraid that he might have dragged the body down the stairs.

She locked the door carefully and followed him to the kitchen, where he was returning the gloves to their place under the sink.

"What did you find? Tell me everything you

found. Warn me if there are any gross parts so that I can steel myself."

J.P. laid the three envelopes in a row on the kitchen table. He sat down and closed his eyes. "I have to reconstruct everything by seeing it again in my mind," he explained.

"I'm going to take notes. We need it all written down," said Caroline. She sat down across from him with her pencil and paper.

"Okay. Here goes. First, it's just a studio apartment—just one big room, with a little kitchen area, and a separate bathroom. In the main room it's just your standard stuff. A couch—I think the couch must open into a bed—and a coffee table and a couple of chairs. By the window, there's another table and a chair. He's not very neat. There's a dirty shirt hanging over the back of one chair—"

"What do you mean, 'dirty'?" asked Caroline. Her pencil was poised over the paper, but she hadn't written anything down yet. "Bloodstains?"

J.P. shook his head. His eyes were still closed. "No, just dirty like it needs to go to the laundry.

There's a cup half-filled with cold coffee on the table by the window. Also on that table is a typewriter and some books and yesterday's newspaper and the letter you read, the one from the agent that says not to use cyanide."

Caroline wrote that down. "Cyanide letter. Evidence number one."

"One of the books was a dictionary," J.P. went on, with his forehead wrinkled as he strained in his photographic memory to see the titles. "And one was *History of Baseball,* and one was *Forensic Toxicology*—"

"Poison book," said Caroline, writing it. "Evidence number two. It's way overdue at the library by now."

"—and the last book was *Yeats: The Complete Poems.*"

"Was there a wastebasket?" Caroline asked. "Did you look through his trash?"

J.P. opened his eyes. "Today was trash-collection day. All his wastebaskets were empty, except for the one in the kitchen. I'll get to that. I'm still in the main room."

He closed his eyes again. "A television set. Black and white. On top of the TV was the latest copy of *TV Guide*—"

"Open?"

"Yeah. Open to last night's programs. Just some dumb comedies and *Quincy*."

"*Quincy*," said Caroline. "Crime show. Evidence number three."

"Next, the bathroom," said J.P., with his eyes still closed. "Terry cloth bathrobe hanging on a hook on the back of the door. Towel. Sponge. Toothbrush, Aim toothpaste. In the medicine cabinet, a razor—"

"Wait," said Caroline. "Slow down. I want to write that. Razor"—she wrote it—"evidence number four."

J.P. opened his eyes. "Why did you write that down?" He reached over and picked up a piece of chicken.

"You can kill someone with a razor."

"Not with that kind of razor," said J.P. with his mouth full. "It was a twenty-nine-cent Bic."

"I bet you could if you tried real hard. What else was in the medicine cabinet?"

J.P. licked his fingers and closed his eyes again. "Aspirin, mouthwash, and—here's something, Caroline. Powder. Write that down."

"Powder? Why?"

"I dumped some in the first envelope. It can be analyzed. The can just said Baby Powder, but that could be a fake. *Arsenic* is a white powder."

Caroline wrote, *Arsnick. Powder. Evidence #5.* She looked up. "How do you know that, J.P.?"

He shrugged. "Everybody knows that," he said. He opened his eyes and took another piece of chicken. "Don't touch those envelopes. They could be lethal."

Caroline glanced at the three white envelopes. Two were bulky and bulging, and the third—obviously the one that held the Baby Powder Arsenic—was flat. "Is that all for the bathroom?" she asked.

Her brother nodded. "Now the kitchen." He closed his eyes again. "Refrigerator: two beers—"

"Wait," said Caroline. "Alcoholism," she said, scribbling. "Evidence number six."

"—half of a pizza with pepperoni. A dozen eggs. Chunk of cheese with mold on it—"

"Wait. Is mold poison?"

"No. It just *looks* poisonous. Refrigerator, continued: half a pound of butter. Wilted lettuce. And some hamburger."

"That's it?"

"That's it for the refrigerator. Moving along now to the cupboards. Mostly bare. Just a few dishes and some canned soup. The wastebasket—"

"Yeah, the wastebasket. That's important."

"A crumpled paper towel and a crushed beer can."

"Wait." Caroline moved her pencil back to #6 and added a word. *SEVERE Alcoholism,* it said now. "Do you think I should put 'inhuman strength'? Because of the crushed beer can?"

J.P. opened his eyes and gave her a disgusted look. "*Anybody* can crush a beer can, Caroline. A small *baby* could crush a beer can."

Caroline shrugged. "What else? What's in those other two envelopes?"

He closed his eyes once more. "Under the sink —write this down, Caroline: rubber gloves."

Caroline sat there with her pencil poised. "What's

wrong with rubber gloves?" she asked. "Mom has rubber gloves."

"These are pink," said J.P., his eyes still closed.

"So?"

"So a man would never buy pink rubber gloves. No man in his right mind would buy pink rubber gloves—not unless he needed them for sinister reasons."

That made sense to Caroline. "Oh," she said. "Fingerprint-proof gloves," she said. "Evidence number seven."

"I took one of the gloves," J.P. said. "It's in the second envelope."

"What about the third?"

J.P. grinned without opening his eyes. "We're still under the sink. Ivory Liquid. SOS pads. Ajax."

"Ajax is a white powder. Could it be arsenic too?"

J.P. shook his head. "It really smelled like Ajax. Anyway, there wouldn't be any way to get it into the can. You'd have to put it in through all the little holes."

"What's in the third envelope, J.P.?"

He paused dramatically. "The corpus," he said.

"The what?"

J.P. grinned again and opened his eyes. "You said we needed a corpus? So I found us a corpus. Dead mouse, still in the trap!"

Caroline jumped up from her chair and looked at the third bulky envelope. "Yuck!" she said. "Did you have to bring it home?"

"What good is evidence if you don't *have* it? And it's kind of cute. It has a pink nose."

Evidence #8, corpus, wrote Caroline, making a face.

J.P. opened his eyes and reached for the last piece of chicken. "This chicken sucks," he said. "It's ice cold."

After they had dumped the remains of the TV dinners in the trash and eaten some ice cream, Caroline looked again at the envelopes of evidence. "What are we going to do with this stuff, J.P.?"

"Save it to show the police. They'll have to analyze it in their lab."

"But where can we keep it? Tomorrow's cleaning day. I suppose I have some secret places in my room, but I don't want the corpus in my room—it'll smell."

"How about the freezer?"

"Mom would see it."

"What about inside that big vase on the table by the front door?"

Caroline eyed the vase and shook her head. "Every now and then she washes that. Maybe she'll decide to wash it tomorrow."

"I could fit it inside the back of the TV, I think. But when the TV's on, it gets warm in there. We might end up with roasted corpus," said J.P.

"Yuck. Wait," said Caroline. "I have an idea. Let me see if they're still there." She went to the closet by the front door and pushed through the winter coats. She shoved the vacuum cleaner aside. "Here they are! This'll be perfect!"

She pulled them out and held them up triumphantly: two galoshes, huge, with flapping buckles.

"Where did those come from?" asked J.P., looking at them with disdain.

"That guy left them here. The one who was the Scrabble expert. Mom was going to give them to

Goodwill, but she never did. Every time she gets out the vacuum cleaner, she says, 'I ought to get rid of those awful things.' But then she forgets about them again. Put the evidence in one of these and I'll stick them way back in the farthest corner of the closet."

J.P. gave it some thought, nodded finally, and deposited the three envelopes in one of the galoshes. He buckled it all the way up, and Caroline carried it between two fingers back to the closet.

"There," she said. "Arsenic, killer's glove, and a corpus with a pink nose. Safely stashed." She closed the closet door.

"Nine o'clock," she said, looking at her watch. "I'm going to watch *Movie of the Week*—it's a dinosaur picture. Hollywood makes such disgusting dinosaurs. They can't tell a Brachiosaurus from an Iguanodon, those jerks."

"Oh, no, you're not," said J.P., leaping toward the television. "I'm watching a special on another channel. Mom promised me I could."

"Liar! You never even asked her! I've been planning all week to watch that dinosaur movie!"

Caroline tried to grab his hand away from the channel knob. But J.P. was stronger than she. He had his hand locked in place. "No fair, you beastly creep!"

When Joanna Tate arrived home at ten, Caroline and J.P. were still locked in warfare. They had flicked the channels back and forth so often that the picture on the screen was just a maze of zigzag lines, and the sound was a staticky buzz. J.P.'s shirt was torn where Caroline had wrenched at his arm, and his sneakers were lying in separate corners of the living room; he had thrown them at her.

"Well," said their mother, "it's another placid evening at the civilized Tate residence."

"I brought you something," Mrs. Tate said, after she had taken off her jacket, "and you don't deserve it, either one of you, since you've wrecked the television once again—"

"I can fix it, Mom," J.P. muttered angrily.

"What did you bring us?" asked Caroline.

"Actually it wasn't me. It was Fred. He felt bad that you guys were home all alone—he said we should have taken you with us for dinner. I didn't explain to him that you tend to behave like a couple of prehistoric beasts—"

"Mom," warned Caroline, "watch what you say about prehistoric—"

"Sorry, I lost my head. Anyway, just as we were leaving the restaurant, he said, 'Wait a minute,' and he went back and got you these. Here. You don't deserve them. But here they are anyway. Cannolis."

She put a paper bag on the coffee table. Neither Caroline nor J.P. moved.

"Well?" said their mother. "I know you love cannolis. Maybe some sweets will soothe your rotten tempers."

Caroline opened the top of the bag, using her fingers fastidiously, like tweezers. Suspiciously she lifted out the two thick pastries dusted with sugar. She looked at her brother meaningfully. J.P. leaned over and sniffed the powdery coating.

"Smells like sugar," he murmured.

"Of course it smells like sugar," said Joanna Tate. "It *is* sugar. Your dental bills will be higher than usual. But what the heck; it was nice of him to think of you. Dig in."

"Mom," asked Caroline, "did you say he went back in and got these? After you had already left the restaurant?"

"Yes. Why?"

"Well, ah, did you go back in with him? Or did you wait outside? Did you *see* the restaurant people putting these in the bag?"

Her mother looked at her, puzzled. "I waited outside. I was reading the menu pasted on the window. I was wondering if I should have ordered the spaghetti with clam sauce. I *liked* the spaghetti with sausage and mushrooms, but the clam sauce looked so good. The people at the next table had it. Next time, I think— *Why,* Caroline? Why did you ask that?"

"Oh," said Caroline vaguely, staring at the cannolis, "I was just thinking that it really isn't safe for a woman to stand around alone on the sidewalk in New York late at night. You should have gone back in with him."

"Caroline, you're becoming downright para-noid. You call and ask if I have the door locked, and you— Why aren't you guys eating those cannolis?" Joanna Tate looked from Caroline to J.P. and back to Caroline again. "What's the matter?"

"Nothing," said Caroline hastily. "They really look like great cannolis. I've never seen them with quite that much sugar on top before."

"Yeah," said J.P. "All that sugar. Yum." He sniffed the cannolis again. He looked at Caroline and raised one eyebrow.

"I'm going to go put my bathrobe on," said their mother. "After you eat those, maybe you could repair the television, J.P.? And we could watch the news?"

She went into the bathroom and closed the door.

"Quick," cried Caroline to her brother. "Get the other galosh."

When their mother came out of the bathroom, wearing her blue quilted robe and with her makeup removed, J.P. was kneeling in front of the TV, work-ing on the dials with a screwdriver. "Almost fixed," he announced.

Caroline was sprawled on the couch, licking

her lips ostentatiously. The coffee table was empty. "Those sure were great cannolis," she said.

Inside the closet, behind the vacuum cleaner, both galoshes were buckled up tight and bulging with evidence.

TWELVE

"I WISH WE HAD a dining room," groaned Caroline early Sunday afternoon. "You should see the Baurichters' dining room. It has thick carpeting and a crystal chandelier and bouquets of fresh flowers everywhere. And silver candlesticks on the table." She looked at their own kitchen table, with its yellow Formica top. "Look at this table. Blecchhh. I wish we didn't have to eat in the kitchen when we have company."

Joanna Tate turned from the sink, where she was washing lettuce, and surveyed the table and Caroline standing beside it, looking depressed. "Well," she suggested, "how about if we move the table into the living room? If we shove the blue wing chair over, it would fit there. Then we could cover it with a tablecloth. And I do have candles. I don't have silver candlesticks, but we can put the candles in—let me think. Here. We can put the candles in these two little juice glasses. How about that?"

She handed Caroline two small glasses that had once had pineapples painted on them. The pineapples were mostly scrubbed away. Caroline stood two yellow candles in the glasses, and brightened. "Yeah," she said. "If I squish them down in hot wax, they'll stand up okay. Thanks. And yes—let's move the table into the living room. That's a neat idea."

They each took an end and maneuvered the table legs around the kitchen door and into the living room. Caroline shoved the blue chair into a corner, and she and her mother dragged the table to its new spot.

J.P. opened his bedroom door and peered out, frowning. "All that thumping and crashing is messing up my electronic work," he complained. He looked at the table. "What are you guys doing? You're not going to wax the kitchen floor again, are you? You waxed it last year."

"Nope," said his mother. "We're going to dine graciously tonight. Here, Caroline: a tablecloth." She took a white embroidered cloth from a drawer and tossed it to Caroline. "Candlelight too, J.P. A real honest-to-goodness dinner party."

J.P. leaned on his bedroom door and watched as Caroline straightened the cloth on the table. He made a face. "Can I eat in my room?"

"Absolutely not. You're going to eat here, and you're going to use decent manners," said his mother. She stood back and admired the effect of the tablecloth. "I wish we had flowers," she said.

"I hate everyone who's coming," announced J.P., swinging his bedroom door back and forth.

"You don't even know Mr. Keretsky," Caroline said angrily. "Mr. Keretsky happens to be a world-renowned scientist."

"Scientist, ha," said J.P. "You call dinosaurs a *science?*"

Caroline grabbed a candle and took aim. "Don't

throw that," warned her mother. "It'll break, and I don't have any others."

"And I hate Stacy Baurichter," J.P. continued, jumping up to grab the top of the door and dangle himself from it. "Stacy Baurichter is a big fake-o jerk."

"Quit doing that to your door," said Joanna Tate. "You'll break the hinges."

"Stacy Baurichter told me that she thinks you're cute," said Caroline sarcastically. "Cute cute cute." She began to fold napkins.

"Liar," muttered J.P. He dangled for a moment and then let himself drop.

"And I expect you both to be polite to Fred Fiske," Mrs. Tate said. "Don't forget to thank him for the cannolis."

"BE POLITE TO WHOM?" asked Caroline, dropping a napkin on the floor.

"Fred Fiske," said her mother. "I invited him to join us. There's plenty of food."

"Oh, *great*," said J.P. "That's just great, Mom. Now I definitely want to eat in my room."

"No way," said Joanna Tate in her don't-argue-with-me voice. "I'm going to finish washing the salad stuff. Caroline, you set the table. For *six*. That's S-I-X. Six." She went to the kitchen.

Glumly Caroline began to put six napkins around the table. J.P. stood in his doorway, watching. "I'm going back to my electronic invention," he said finally. "Because I'm going to use it. *Tonight*."

During the afternoon, after Caroline had set the table for dinner and dusted the living room once more, she helped her mother in the kitchen. Together they baked a chocolate cake and forced each other not to open the oven every five minutes to peek at it. Caroline removed the strings from what seemed fourteen million string beans; she sliced them into a saucepan. "A normal vegetable," she said. "About time."

Her mother peeled potatoes. "Where's J.P.?" she asked. "What's he doing? He usually peels potatoes for me."

"I'll check," said Caroline, and she slid down from the kitchen stool. She went to J.P.'s closed bedroom door and listened. Inside, she could hear mysterious buzzes and crackling noises. She knocked on the door.

"Don't come in," said J.P.

"It's only me," called Caroline softly. "Mom wants to know what you're doing."

J.P. opened the door, motioned her inside, and closed it behind her. On his desk she could see a tangle of wires and switches.

"Look," whispered J.P. He gingerly picked up one green wire with an exposed copper end and touched it to the end of a red wire. Sparks flew, and a tiny column of smoke curled up into the air.

"Zap," muttered J.P. "If you touched that, Caroline, you'd turn into a grilled cheese sandwich."

"I have no intention of touching it," she replied, moving farther away from his desk. "What are you going to do with it?"

"Show me which chair Fiske is going to sit in at dinner," he said. "I'm going to wire it. It'll be a do-it-yourself electric chair."

Caroline backed away even farther. "Oh, no, you're not," she said. "No way. You're not going to kill anybody at my dinner party. Not even that Tyrannosaurus Frederick Fiske."

J.P. looked at her impatiently. "Of course I'm not going to kill him, stupid; do you think I'm crazy? I don't have enough juice to kill him, anyway. I'm just going to *stun* him. Then, when he's stunned, sitting there helpless and stupefied, we'll confront him with all the evidence—in front of witnesses—and we'll call the police."

"But, J.P., it's a dinner party! It's going to be gracious dining, with candles and everything! Couldn't you do it another time?"

J.P.'s voice was determined. "How many chances do you think we'll get, Caroline? His deadline's the first of May—you know that."

He opened his door and peeked out. "How long will Mom be in the kitchen?" he whispered.

"A while. The cake's almost done, and then we have to make the frosting."

"You keep her in there, okay? And show me which is his chair."

Reluctantly Caroline pointed through the crack

in the door. "The one at the end. Opposite Mom. You and Stacy will be on the side by the wall, and I'll sit with Mr. Keretsky on the other side."

J.P. eyed the distance between his door and the chair where Frederick Fiske would sit. "Okay," he said. "Got it."

"J.P.—"

He interrupted her. "Make sure Mom stays in the kitchen while I wire the chair."

"Does it have to be during the dinner party?" Caroline almost wailed. "We're having mashed potatoes and chocolate cake and—"

"I won't do it till the end of dessert," J.P. said. "If you're sure it's chocolate cake."

Caroline trudged back to the kitchen. "Cake should be done, Mom," she announced with phony cheerfulness. "Tell me how to start making frosting. And you stay right here and watch me, okay? I don't want to mess it up."

Glancing behind her, she could see J.P. on all fours, crawling from his room to Frederick Fiske's chair with some wires in his hand.

• • •

Gregor Keretsky was the first to arrive. Caroline met him downstairs at the front door and nodded when he asked in a low, concerned voice, "Is this necktie all right?"

"Brown and beige, with some yellow squiggles," she told him. "It will go with the candles."

He was carrying a bouquet of daisies. "For me?" asked Caroline in delight.

"No," he said, smiling. "For your mama. Because she is so kind to invite me for dinner. For you I have something else, something special." He patted the pocket of his jacket.

Mrs. Tate arranged the flowers on the table with pleasure, after she had been introduced to Mr. Keretsky. "Look," she said. "Don't they look beautiful with the yellow candles?"

Gregor Keretsky just smiled. When Joanna Tate had turned away, he winked at Caroline and shrugged. It was their secret: that the flowers, the candles, even his necktie, were all simply gray to him.

It's nice to have a secret with someone, she thought. Then she cringed, thinking of the secret she had with J.P. At the foot of Frederick Fiske's chair, curled unobtrusively around the metal leg, was a knotted ball of wires; from there they went under the rug and reappeared again on the floor leading into her brother's bedroom.

And now she had *another* awful secret, this one with her mother, who had made her promise not to tell. When they'd been frosting the cake together, her mother had whispered, "Guess what, Caroline. I have an absolute, full-fledged, *major* crush on Frederick Fiske."

Caroline had continued to swirl chocolate frosting around the sides of the cake. Her heart sank. She managed a small half-smile.

"You know the fifty-third thing I love about you, Caroline?" asked her mother happily. "You're so inscrutable."

Caroline didn't even know what *inscrutable* meant. But she was fairly certain it didn't mean someone who was planning to turn her mother's heartthrob into a grilled cheese sandwich.

Mrs. Tate was pouring Gregor Keretsky a glass of wine when the front doorbell buzzed again, and Caroline ran downstairs to let Stacy in.

"Comes by Bus, Leaves by Cab," Stacy announced. "I promised my mom that I'd get a taxi home, because it'll be dark." They bounded up the stairs together. "What's for dinner? And is your brother going to be here?"

J.P. came out of his bedroom when Stacy arrived. To her surprise, Caroline saw that he was wearing his sports jacket and his only necktie. "All of a sudden there's a dress code for electronic events?" she murmured in his ear as she passed him on the way to the kitchen. But J.P. paid no attention. He also paid no attention to Mr. Keretsky, beyond a polite how-do-you-do. He paid a *lot* of attention to Stacy Baurichter, who began to giggle and fool with her hair.

Finally there was a knock on the door, and Frederick Fiske was there. In unison, after the introductions, Caroline and J.P. said politely, "Thank you for the cannolis, Mr. Fiske." Caroline added meaningfully, "We both ate them Friday night." They watched his face.

He'll squirm uncomfortably, thought Caroline. He'll wonder why we're not dead. There was enough arsenic on the cannolis to kill a Triceratops.

But Frederick Fiske didn't squirm at all. He grinned and said, "I'm glad you liked them."

He had brought a bottle of wine as a gift. Caroline thought briefly that she should change her list of evidence to read *VERY SEVERE Alcoholism*, but the list had been stuffed into one of the galoshes, on top of the cannolis. And, of course, her very own mother and Gregor Keretsky were sipping wine as well.

She would bring out the list when the police arrived. Frederick Fiske would be stunned by then, dazed and stupefied; probably she and J.P. should tie him up. Then the police would come. She would present the list and the evidence itself: the cannolis dusted with poison, which could go to the lab for analysis; the arsenic that had been cleverly hidden in Fiske's baby powder can; the sinister pink rubber glove, probably filled on the inside with Frederick Fiske's fingerprints; the damning notes from the secret agent; and of course the corpus delicti, which probably still had poison on its tiny whiskers.

Suddenly she noticed that J.P. was inching closer to her on the couch. The adults were all talking about what a lovely spring day it had been. Stacy was listening politely and nodding, and inch by inch J.P. was moving over toward Caroline until he was close enough to whisper in her ear.

"He's not going to be grounded," J.P. said in a very low and very perturbed voice.

Caroline looked at him, puzzled. "Of course he's not going to be grounded," she whispered back. "He's going to be electrocuted. You and me, J.P., *we're* going to be grounded—probably for months—if this scheme doesn't work right."

J.P. shook his head impatiently. "He's not going to be grounded electrically, because he has rubber soles on his shoes," he muttered. "I don't think the zap will work unless he takes his shoes off." He sidled back to his place on the couch and smiled politely at everyone.

Caroline frowned. Maybe, she thought, it would be just as well if the zap didn't work. Then this pleasant dinner party wouldn't be disrupted by police, and they could all have second helpings of chocolate cake, and—

No, she thought. Fiske will find a way to sprinkle

poison on my cake and J.P.'s. Maybe he'll even do Stacy's. The agent said to eliminate the kids. Even though he's sitting there posing as Mr. Nice Guy, and even though my mother has a full-fledged crush on him, and even though he seems to like her a whole lot and maybe even regrets by now that he has to eliminate the kids—still, he's under orders. If we don't zap him tonight, he'll still be at large, and his deadline is May first, and he probably has poison in his pocket, ready to use.

"It's such a warm night," Caroline said aloud. "I guess I'll take off my shoes. Maybe we'd all be more comfortable with our shoes off. What do you think, J.P.?" She kicked off her sandals and wiggled her bare toes. Her mother gave her a very dirty look.

"Good idea," said J.P. loudly. He pried off his dress shoes, one after the other. "Stacy? Everybody?"

Stacy giggled. "Sure, J.P.," she said. "You have great ideas." Stacy untied her shoes and took them off.

The adults were all looking at them curiously. Finally Joanna Tate said, in a flustered voice, "Well, the forty-third thing I love about Caroline is that

168

she's sometimes completely unpredictable. Just when I'm feeling very proud of her good manners, she surprises me by doing something very strange. J.P., too." She glared at Caroline and J.P.

Caroline ignored the glare. This is for your own good, Mom, she thought. You will thank me for this.

"Mr. Keretsky?" said Caroline. "Wouldn't you like to take your shoes off, too?" She looked very meaningfully at Gregor Keretsky. He looked a little confused. He stared at Caroline; then he stared at his shoes, as if there might be some explanation there. He hitched up his trouser legs a little and peered at his shoes with a quizzical frown.

Stacy began to laugh. Then Joanna Tate started to laugh. Frederick Fiske chuckled.

"Forgive me, Mr. Keretsky," Caroline's mother said. "I shouldn't laugh. But do you know that you're wearing one blue sock and one green one?"

Gregor Keretsky grinned sheepishly. "Ah, Caroline," he said with a sigh, "my darkest secret is exposed."

From the kitchen, the timer on the stove buzzed.

"Dinner's ready," Joanna Tate said, standing up. "Caroline, will you come and help me in the kitchen? J.P., will you show everyone to their seats? And both of you—you too, Stacy—will you kindly put your shoes back on?"

Caroline leaned over to put on her sandals and whispered to J.P., who was forcing his feet back into his own shoes, "This is going to be a horrible evening. Horrible horrible horrible."

Stacy had retied her shoes. She stood up. "Kids Re-shod," she announced, "Meal Begins."

THIRTEEN

OUTSIDE, THE SPRING EVENING had turned from pink and gold to a dark, threatening night. Thunder rumbled across the city.

Joanna Tate refilled the adults' wineglasses and got up to close the windows. "It's raining," she said. "So much for the beautiful spring weather."

"April showers," said Frederick Fiske.

"Nope," announced Joanna Tate. "April downpour."

"When I was in London last week," said Gregor Keretsky, "it rained both days." He looked up suddenly and smiled. "That reminds me! I brought Caroline a small gift from my conference. You will forgive me if I make this little presentation during dinner?"

Everyone nodded and watched curiously as he removed a little packet from the inside pocket of his suit coat. He grinned proudly. "For most of you, this will seem a strange gift, I think. But for Caroline, I hope it will be a treasure." Meticulously he unwrapped the bit of folded paper and then held up a tiny, gray, mottled object. He handed it to Caroline, who took it carefully and held it in the palm of her open hand.

"What is it — a *rock?*" asked Stacy, peering across the table.

Caroline grinned and shook her head. She knew it wasn't a rock.

"It's a chip of a mastodon bone," Gregor Keretsky explained. "Radiocarbon dates it about one and a half million years ago."

"Early Pleistocene," breathed Caroline, in awe. She turned it over and over in her hand.

"A glacial period," Gregor Keretsky explained.

"New York was probably covered with ice when this mastodon lived."

"Even the Empire State Building?" asked Stacy, reaching for some more string beans.

Everyone laughed, even Stacy, after she had thought for a moment. "Someday we'll all be extinct," said Frederick Fiske. "Someday I suppose scientists will be digging up *our* bones."

His voice, and what he had said, brought Caroline back to reality from the Early Pleistocene Age. You first, she thought; you're going to be extinct before I am, Frederick Fiske. J.P. and I are going to see to that as soon as we finish the dessert.

"Well," said Joanna Tate, "this leg of lamb is extinct. I guess it's time for chocolate cake."

"Mom," said Caroline, "you stay right in your seat. J.P. and I can clear the table and serve the cake." Carefully she put the mastodon bone into the pocket of her skirt. "Thank you, Mr. Keretsky. It's the best gift anyone ever gave me."

She and her brother conferred in the kitchen as they scraped the bits of food from the plates into the garbage disposal. Lightning streaked across the sky outside and was followed by heavy, shuddering thunder.

"Good night for a murder," Caroline remarked, shivering. She nibbled at a string bean that Stacy had left on her plate. "Keep your eye on Fiske in case he tries to sprinkle poison on our dessert."

J.P. was sulking. "I can't zap him, Caroline, unless he takes off his shoes. I spent all afternoon rigging up that zapper, and then he wore rubber-soled shoes, the jerk."

Caroline sliced the chocolate cake carefully and put it on plates. She could hear her mother and the company talking and laughing in the other room.

"I have an idea," she said slowly, watching the rain splatter against the kitchen window. "I think I can get his shoes off."

"How?" J.P.'s eyes brightened.

"Never mind. It's too complicated to describe. You just be ready. When we're almost finished with dessert, you watch me. I'll get Fiske's shoes off—for a minute, at least; the timing will have to be perfect—and you press your switch when I say 'Now.'"

"It's not a switch; it's a button. I've got it all rigged

on the floor. I press the button with my foot, and it activates the wire to his chair leg, which activates the wire attached to the flat bottom of Mom's old iron, which I slipped in through the ripped part of the chair seat so that it's right under his butt, and the whole thing's attached to my old Lionel train transformer in my room, and—"

"Skip the details. I don't understand electricity, anyway. Here—take some of these plates in."

Caroline and J.P. served the cake and poured coffee for the adults. As Caroline leaned over Stacy to put her plate down, Stacy whispered, "He doesn't seem like a crazed killer. I think he's kind of nice."

"Wait till you see all the evidence laid out. Later," Caroline whispered back.

Caroline watched all the plates. Gregor Keretsky ate his cake slowly, savoring each bite. "This is wonderful," he said. "Caroline, your mama said you helped her make this cake. Maybe you should become a chef instead of a paleontologist?"

His eyes were twinkling. Caroline knew he was only joking.

Stacy nibbled at her cake, fastidiously wiping

crumbs from her mouth with her napkin. "I'm really interested in the Computer Club at school, J.P.," she was saying. "What exactly do you do?"

Caroline groaned to herself. She knew Stacy didn't give a hoot about the Computer Club. What Stacy was interested in, all of a sudden, was Caroline's brother. She was going to have to have a serious talk with Stacy. Once a woman got involved with the opposite sex, her whole future career could go down the drain.

Frederick Fiske was also devouring his cake enthusiastically, and his plate was almost empty. He was scraping up the last bits of frosting with his fork. It was time. She glanced meaningfully at J.P.

Caroline took a deep breath. If her plan didn't work, she didn't have any alternative plan in mind, and the whole thing would be a horrible failure. Horrible horrible horrible.

She took a big bite of cake. Then she said, "This cake makes me very thirsty." With her left hand she picked up her glass of milk and took a swallow. Still holding the glass of milk, she took her mastodon bone out of her pocket.

"This is such a wonderful gift, Mr. Keretsky," she said.

She glanced up to be sure that J.P. was watching. She dropped the small chip of bone on the floor. "Whoops!" she said. "I dropped it!" Everyone, including J.P., looked a little startled.

"Excuse me, everyone," Caroline said. "I know it's rude to crawl under the table, but I don't want to lose my mastodon bone."

Still holding her glass of milk, she knelt on the floor and then disappeared under the tablecloth.

"Don't move your feet, anyone!" she called in a commanding voice. "I don't want anyone to step on the mastodon bone!"

Quickly she returned the chip of bone to her pocket. No matter what else happened, she wasn't going to sacrifice the mastodon bone. Caroline glanced around at the pairs of feet under the table. There were Mr. Keretsky's, with their unmatched socks. There were her mother's, in dark brown high-heeled shoes. There were Stacy's, curled around the rung of her chair. There were J.P.'s best shoes, and beside them, with wires running from it, was a small button that looked like a discarded doorbell. J.P.'s left foot moved and arranged itself over the button in pushing position.

And there were Frederick Fiske's feet in their rubber-soled loafers. For an eerie instant she wondered whether, with his shoes off, he would reveal huge scaly feet with long curved nails, like those of a Tyrannosaurus.

But she didn't hesitate. She poured her glass of milk over both of Frederick Fiske's feet, carefully including his socks. He jumped.

"Sorry!" called Caroline from under the table. "Don't get up, Mr. Fiske. By mistake I spilled my milk. Here, let me help you get your shoes off so I can dry them with my napkin!" She grabbed one of his feet so that he couldn't stand up, and in an instant she had both of his loafers off.

"NOW, J.P.!" she yelled. And her brother's foot came down hard on the button.

There was a loud buzzing noise, a flash of sparks, and everything went dark.

• • •

Caroline groped her way through the maze of human legs and the folds of the tablecloth. She re-emerged into a room that was totally dark except for the two small sputtering candles on the table. She looked at the dim figures seated around the table, expecting to see Frederick Fiske slumped in his chair, zapped and stunned.

But Frederick Fiske was laughing. He was bending over to mop at his wet socks with his napkin.

"What on earth happened?" asked Joanna Tate. "Where are the lights?"

"It must be the storm," explained Gregor Keretsky. He stood up and looked through the window, out into the rainy street. "The streetlights are on. And the lights in other buildings. Could it be maybe just a fuse?"

Caroline peered through the darkness at J.P. He was sitting silently, with his head in his hands. "I blew it," she could hear him mutter.

"Well," said Frederick Fiske, standing up, "I can squish down the stairs to the basement, I guess, and see if I can find the fuse box." He went to the door of the apartment, stumbling into a chair in the darkness, and opened it. They could hear him speak to someone in the pitch-black hall. In a moment he was back.

"Jason Carruthers is going down," he said. "All the lights are off in the whole building. He's going to find a flashlight and check out the wiring in the basement. He said we should just sit tight."

Sure we'll sit tight, thought Caroline. Here we are in a dark room with a murderer, a thunderstorm outside, two candles that are just about to go out, and no other candles in the house.

I want my Stegosaurus, she thought suddenly. I want my stuffed Stegosaurus.

Then she reached into her pocket, remembering her mastodon bone. She held it tightly in her hand and found that it was just as comforting as the stuffed animal on her closet shelf.

One of the candles, no more than a stub now, flickered and went out. "LIGHT FAILS," headlined Stacy, a little nervously. Outside another roar of thunder rumbled across the sky; heavy sheets of rain washed against the windows in the gusty wind.

The last candle flared briefly, hissed, and went out. Now the room was completely dark.

"I think," said Joanna Tate cheerfully, "that we should have a conversation. It's a little spooky, sitting here without saying anything."

"Not spooky," said Gregor Keretsky. "It's cozy, being with other people. Most nights I am alone in my little apartment. For me it is more pleasant to be with friends, even in the dark, than to be alone with bright lights on. Don't you think so, Caroline?" Through the darkness he reached over and took Caroline's hand. Now she had the mastodon bone in one hand and Gregor Keretsky's firm hand in her other. She felt better, less terrified.

"I guess so," she said uncertainly.

"Mr. Keretsky," asked Stacy, "why do you live all alone? Don't you have a family?"

He was silent for a minute. He sighed and shifted in his chair, still grasping Caroline's hand. "I don't want to tell a sad story on such a pleasant night," he said. "So I will tell only a little of what happened to me, and you must not let it make you feel sad, because it is many years ago, and now you see how things are: we are all happy here together!

"When I was a young man—you will never believe this, Caroline, but it is true—I was a painter. I was not a *great* painter, but I was a *good* one, I think. This was in Europe. And then, in Europe, came the war.

"Now, I am not going to talk about the war, because you all know that war is a bad time. I lost my family."

Caroline held tightly to his hand. "Did you have children?" she asked.

He cleared his throat. "A little girl. She was about your age, Caroline, though she was not as —what would the word be?—incorrigible? I don't mean that as a bad thing. In fact, if I may borrow your mama's way of speaking, it is the ninety-fourth thing that I love about Caroline, I think: that she is incorrigible."

"Me too," said Joanna Tate from the end of the table.

Gregor Keretsky went on. "Now, that was the sad thing, that my family—my parents, my wife, my daughter—were gone. But it is long ago, and I will not dwell upon that. I will tell you of the other thing that I lost. Can you guess what it is, Caroline?"

She nodded in the dark. "Colors," she said, squeezing his hand. "You lost colors. I think that's *very* sad."

"I thought so, too, at the time, because of course I could never paint again. But as I told you, I was not a great painter. The doctors could find no reason that my colors had disappeared. They wrote about me, in journals and medical books.

"I had to find another profession. And this is the happy part. I had always been interested in science, and so I went back to the university, and after a long time of study I became a paleontologist. The bones I study—like your little mastodon chip, Caroline —have no colors. We don't have any way to know what color the great beasts were. Maybe the mastodon was pink? Yellow?"

Caroline giggled, picturing a Walt Disney version

of the mastodon. "Blue with yellow polka dots?" she suggested.

"Perhaps," said Gregor Keretsky. "We will never know. And this is my story: why I have no family, Stacy; why I am a paleontologist instead of a painter; and why, even, I have a funny pair of socks. You see it is a story with a happy ending, even though there are sad parts to it."

"Maybe all of our stories are similar," suggested Joanna Tate. "I always wanted to be a poet. Instead, I'm a bank teller. I would never have been a *great* poet —"

"You're a good poet, Mom," said Caroline defensively.

Her mother laughed. "Well, I'm a better bank teller. And who knows? Maybe someday I'll be a bank president!"

"I never wanted to be anything but a paleontologist," said Caroline. "And I will be a paleontologist, I'm sure of it."

"I'm sure of it, too," said Gregor Keretsky.

"And me," said Stacy from her side of the table,

"I've always wanted to be an investigative journalist. I will be, too: the best one in the whole world!"

"Good for you, Stacy," said Gregor Keretsky. "And how about you, J.P.? You are sitting so quietly."

Caroline couldn't see J.P. through the darkness —only his outline—but she could tell that his head was still in his hands. He lifted it at Mr. Keretsky's question.

"I don't know," J.P. said gloomily. "I always thought I was an electronics expert. But right now I'm beginning to wonder."

Frederick Fiske had been silent. She could see the outline of his tall figure, so Caroline knew that he was still there, but he hadn't said a word. Now he finally spoke.

"I have very wet feet," he said. "No offense, Caroline; I know it was an accident. But they're beginning to get cold. Maybe it will take my mind off them if I tell you *my* story."

"Tate Spills Milk: Fiske Spills Beans," announced Stacy.

"Right," said Frederick Fiske. "I'm going to spill

the beans. I'm involved in a project, and up till now I haven't told anyone."

Caroline edged nervously away from Frederick Fiske, closer to Gregor Keretsky. She shuddered. Outside, the growling thunder and the drenching rain continued relentlessly.

Fourteen

"Is there any more coffee, by any chance?" asked Frederick Fiske.

"A little," said Joanna Tate, "but it's probably not hot, since the electricity's off. Here, I'll get you some, if you don't mind lukewarm."

They could hear her fumble in the darkness, groping her way to the coffeepot. "Ouch," she said as she bumped into a chair. "Hope I don't miss your cup. I can barely see."

She poured the last of the coffee into Frederick Fiske's cup and then pulled up a chair next to his.

"I'm not going to try to find my way back to the other end of the table," she said. "I'm already covered with bruises."

Frederick Fiske sipped and spoke. "As I've told your mother, I teach at Columbia. Professor of history. Not a *great* professor of history," he added, chuckling, "but a good one.

"I'd been teaching there for fifteen years. Teaching the same stuff year after year, and frankly—I hope you don't mind the analogy, Gregor—it was beginning to lose its color for me. I was bored.

"I lived up near Columbia, on Riverside Drive— by myself; I've never been married—and last year, in the evenings, when I should have been correcting papers, I found that I was jotting down notes and ideas for a novel. I've always been a great reader."

"Me too," said Stacy.

"Me too," said Joanna Tate.

"Shhh," said Caroline. "I want to hear what comes next."

"Well, this novel that was beginning to take shape in my head and in my notes had nothing at all to do with history. You'd think that with my background—I have a Ph.D. in medieval history, after all—"

"An interesting period, the medieval," said Gregor Keretsky.

"Not as interesting as the Mesozoic," Caroline reminded him.

"Shhh," said J.P. "I want to hear what comes next."

"It's very contemporary. And—this is kind of embarrassing—it's a thriller. A spy novel. It has all kinds of murder—right now I'm doing research on obscure poisons—and, of course, it includes, excuse me, sex."

"Of course," said Stacy. "That's essential."

"Shhh," said Gregor Keretsky. "I want to hear what comes next."

"Well, I won't try to retell the plot, because it's so terribly convoluted. But it really seemed pretty good, at least to me. So last year I wrote up a whole outline and a couple of chapters and a synopsis of some other chapters, and I sent it all to an agent."

"Carl Broderick," said Stacy and Caroline in unison.

"Yes," said Frederick Fiske in a puzzled voice. "How on earth did you know that?"

They were both silent. "Lucky guess," Caroline finally mumbled.

"Shhh," said J.P. "Go on, Mr. Fiske. What happened?"

"Broderick thought it was terrific. He took it to a publisher, and the publisher thought it was terrific. They gave me a contract.

"But it was, as I said, a little embarrassing. There I was in this very academic community, which looks down its nose at popular novels. So I didn't tell anyone I was doing it. Finally it became so time-consuming that I took a year's leave of absence from Columbia, secretly rented this apartment, and holed up to finish the writing. All my colleagues think I'm in France, doing some research on the extortionate taxes in Paris in 1437."

"Sounds boring," said J.P.

"Shhh," said Caroline.

"Well, that's about it. The novel's done, and I'm working on revisions—I have to have them finished by May first, so time's getting a little tight. But Broderick's already shown the manuscript to some movie people, and there's a good chance that the film rights will be sold. There's a rumor that Dustin Hoffman wants to play the lead character.

"You know a funny thing?" Frederick Fiske went on. "Tonight was a big help to me."

"You have a scene where an electronics expert short-circuits a whole house?" asked J.P.

"One of your characters dumps a glass of milk on somebody's feet?" asked Caroline.

"No." He laughed. "I've had this odd problem with the writing. There are some kids in the novel —they're not major characters, but I liked having them in there. But I don't have any children myself. I don't *know* any children; at least, I didn't until tonight. And I just couldn't make those kids in the book come to life."

"So you killed them, right?" asked Stacy ominously.

"No." He chuckled again. "But Carl Broderick finally said I'd have to eliminate them. I've been going through the whole book, trying to take out the kids every place they appear. It's been driving me crazy."

"How did tonight help?" asked Caroline.

He thought for a moment. "Well, I was thinking of kids as some kind of separate creatures, as if they were different in some way from adults. Tonight, watching you three, listening to you, I realized that there isn't any difference."

"We're just shorter," said J.P.

"Right. But you think and joke and react and talk like ordinary people. Now I can go back upstairs to my typewriter and, with any luck and some hard work and long hours, rewrite those kids so they'll be real."

"Not if it's an electric typewriter, you can't," said J.P. in a discouraged voice. "We may never have juice in this building again."

Just then the lights came on. Everybody blinked.

Caroline blinked twice, after she had looked around the table. Next to her was Gregor Keretsky, relaxed and smiling, with his hand still cupped around hers. At the end of the table was Frederick

Fiske, and beside him was her mother—and they were holding hands.

Across the table were Stacy and J.P., and both of them moved their hands quickly. Stacy began smoothing her hair, and J.P. folded his napkin, something he had never done before in his entire life. Caroline was almost positive that they, too, had been holding hands in the darkness.

I am going to have to have a very, very serious talk with Stacy Baurichter, thought Caroline.

From the hallway, Jason Carruthers called through the door. "I was able to do a temporary repair job," he said. "And the electricians are coming in the morning."

Stacy looked at her watch. "I have to go," she said. "It's past nine, and it's a school night. But listen, Mr. Fiske, before I go: Do you know the name Harrison Ledyard?"

"Of course," said Frederick Fiske. "He won a Pulitzer Prize last year."

"Well," said Stacy in a voice that Caroline recognized as her fake-sophisticated voice, "I was doing a journalism piece about him. But frankly, he was such

193

a bore that I just dropped the whole idea. Maybe you noticed that *People* magazine ran an article last week on Harrison Ledyard?"

"Yes, I did see it, as a matter of fact," said Frederick Fiske with interest.

"My good friend at *People* magazine, Michael Small, took on the project after I decided that it was excruciatingly boring. But when *your* book comes out, and when Dustin Hoffman gets involved, well, I wonder if you and I could arrange a convenient time for an interview?"

Frederick Fiske grinned. "I'd be honored, Stacy," he said.

"Stacy," said J.P., "I'll go down with you and get you a taxi."

"How about you, Gregor?" asked Joanna Tate. "Do you need a taxi, too?"

"Oh, no," said Gregor Keretsky. "I live only a few short blocks away, down near the museum. I will walk. I don't mind the rain."

"I can loan you an umbrella," said Joanna Tate dubiously. "But the sidewalks and gutters are going to be flooded." She smiled. "I'd hate to see you ruin that extraordinary pair of socks."

"Wet socks aren't so bad," said Frederick Fiske, standing up gingerly, with a squishing sound.

Caroline blushed. "I'm sorry about the milk," she said. "I'm sorry about everything."

Joanna Tate stood up, too. She was looking thoughtfully at Gregor Keretsky's feet. "I just thought of something," she said, and started across the living room. "I used to know this revolting man who was a Scrabble champion. He knew every two-letter word in the dictionary. You couldn't have a conversation with him. He was always muttering, 'Ai, ay, ex, ax, eh, en.' I haven't seen him in months. But he left these here, and I'm sure he'll never be back for them. If they fit—" She headed for the closet.

Oh no, thought Caroline. Please, no.

"MOM," she said loudly, "DO NOT DO WHAT YOU ARE ABOUT TO DO."

Her mother grinned affectionately at her. "The one hundredth thing I love about you, Caroline," she said, "is that sometimes you're completely incomprehensible."

She opened the closet door. "Whew," she said, making a face, "it smells awful in here. I wonder why. Here you go, Gregor—" She reached behind the vacuum cleaner into the dark corner where the galoshes were.

And the rest is too horrible to tell. Horrible horrible horrible.

Just the Tates!

Read all the books about Caroline and J.P.!

There's no one quite like Anastasia!
Enjoy all her antics in the
Anastasia Krupnik series by Lois Lowry!

Move over, Anatasia Krupnik.

It's your little brother Sam's turn to tell his story,
and he's got a lot to say!

More great books by
LOIS LOWRY!

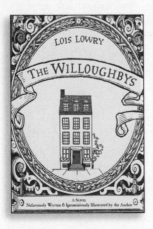